The

Undertaker

The
Undertaker

*A Memoir of the First Woman Funeral
Director in the Core of Brooklyn*

Laura Del Gaudio

GREEN PLACE BOOKS | *Brattleboro, Vermont*

Copyright © 2019 by Laura Del Gaudio

All rights reserved. No part of this book may be reproduced in
any form or by any means, electronic or mechanical, including
photocopying, recording, or by any information storage and retrieval
system, without permission in writing from the publisher.

The Undertakert is a work of nonfiction. Apart from the actual
historic figures, events, and locales that provide background
for the narrative, some of the names, characters, places, and
incidents are products of the author's imagination or are used
fictitiously to bring the historical narrative alive.

Printed in the United States

10 9 8 7 6 5 4 3 2 1

Green Writers Press is a Vermont-based publisher whose mission
is to spread a message of hope and renewal through the words and
images we publish. Throughout we will adhere to our commitment
to preserving and protecting the natural resources of the earth.
To that end, a percentage of our proceeds will be donated to
environmental activist groups and The Southern Poverty Law
Foundation. Green Writers Press gratefully acknowledges support
from individual donors, friends, and readers to help support the
environment and our publishing initiative. Green Place Books
curates books that tell literary and compelling stories with a focus
on writing about place—these books are more personal stories/
memoir and biographies.

GREEN
PLACE
BOOKS

Giving Voice to Writers & Artists Who Will Make the World a Better Place
Green Writers Press | Brattleboro, Vermont
www.greenwriterspress.com

ISBN: 978-1-950584-1-6

COVER DESIGN BY ASHA HOSSAIN DESIGN, LLC

To my son Robert, who leaves me speechless,
Steve Eisner, Maura Burke, and Lisa Brahee
who made it all possible.

There is a crack, a crack in everything.
That's how the light gets in.

—LEONARD COHEN

The
Undertaker

I Was Already Under the Table at Five

A F-A-I-R-L-Y TOLD TALE

ONCE UPON A TIME in the land of "historic" downtown Brooklyn, there was a funeral home known as Del Gaudio and Son. Upstairs in that sturdy, grey and black, castle-like building, I sat under my grandparents' kitchen table and listened intently to the conversations of my family as well as those of the family members of the deceased. On the first floor of this castle, the dead were embalmed, dressed, and made ready for viewing, which took place over two days from 10 a.m. to 10 p.m. with no break. Then, on the third day, the funeral procession occurred.

When I first became aware and stepped back to see what it was I was looking at from under the table, the first thought that came into my head went something like this: *Life ain't no fairy tale.* For some reason, life has always slapped the notion of fairy tales right out of my head. Surrounded by adults, and with two older sisters, fairy tales didn't last too long . . . especially with an uncle illegally running cigarettes up from down South, and another going to jail for forgery.

My Aunt Camy, a tall, handsome woman, would have taken me out with one look if she had ever even heard my thoughts spoken in such clear Italian Brooklynese. She was the one who looked me right in the eye and said, "Chewing gum makes you look like a cow chewing its cud." "*Oh, shoot me now at the thought of it! Please!*" was what I wanted to tell her. But Mom would have come out with her trusty wooden spoon and said, "Come here." Yeah, like that was going to happen. I never once spoke back to Aunt Camy. She commanded genuine respect. I learned not to let any of my Brooklynese thoughts escape, unless they were spoken without offense to the ear when in her company. Forget expressing those thoughts while chewing gum. My greatest fear—being banished to the basement of the funeral home—kept that one in check. I was quite content to sit under the table so I could listen and learn about this *ain't no fairytale* stuff.

Today, in my sixties and getting closer to a procession of my own, I am thinking back to the vital lessons learned about life. My death will be a celebration of life and nothing else, if I can help it. I will tell you where (and how) it all started.

Walking through the front door (not the double doors to our Brooklyn Funeral Home, but the one to the left that led to the apartments) there was, on the right, an open entrance to the funeral home. If you passed that and walked down two steps, there was a long hallway that led straight to the men's room. On the left was a flight of stairs up to the first landing, where the ladies' room was. If you walked around that landing and made another flight of steps, you would find my grandparents' apartment. You could also walk down that hallway and take another flight up to a second apartment. As a child, it seemed to me that the place never ended. I remember the bannisters from the ground floor up were an off-white with every possible color speckle embedded in it. It was fascinating.

When you entered into my grandparents' apartment, you entered a small, darkened foyer. The light was switched on only when the space was in use. On the right was a small wooden desk that held two black rotary phones. One was the house phone; the other was the business phone. There was always a pad of paper and different colored pencils that said *Del Gaudio and Son Funeral Home* on them. I really liked those pencils. The colors made them eye-catching, but I never once took them to school.

Against the far wall stood Grandma's sewing machine. Between the small desk and the sewing machine were two doorways: one to the left that led into the kitchen, and one to the right that led to the living room. It was in the kitchen that I learned about life and death and everything in between, both dark and light. The wall to the right was tiled halfway up with white tiles. A strip of black tiles at the top divided it from the rest of the wall. The floor was white tile also, and very easy to clean. It shone beautifully, especially when the sunlight from the kitchen windows, which were smaller than regular-sized windows, sparkled upon it. I loved it. Now that I think of it, that could have been the beginning of a great surgical room. In any case, all of this made it easy to sit on the floor and try to capture dust particles, but this would become frustrating after a while because it was so difficult.

Opposite the wall I loved were the stove, sink, and counter space, with cabinets underneath. If I climbed up onto the sink and stretched and twisted myself a bit to the left while looking out of those windows, I could see the Statue of Liberty in the distance.

The refrigerator was against the side wall, smack dab in the middle of a series of cabinets that stretched from floor to ceiling. I am sure my father designed and built them. They, too, were white, but would change color from time to time when they needed a paint job. Opposite the refrigerator was a bedroom. I was told that when my sister Rita (my parents' firstborn) was a baby, that doorway held a swing for her.

So there I was, hidden under the table by a variety of different oilcloth tablecloths. Some were checkered black and white, and some yellow. I was safe from being seen unless an adult looked past their knees. The table was large, and it was so easy to sit there . . . and a lot less work than building a fort in the living room. It was also much, much more interesting to listen to the adults than to do battle with make-believe. The table was oblong, and could hold up to ten people.

There were never children for me to play with, ever when I was there. The funeral home was on a business street. People lived above their businesses. The more traffic, the better. It's funny—most young children are afraid of adults. I was afraid of other children, because I could not relate to them. I had no disciplined hour for bedtime. I lived with the freedom of an adult, doing whatever I wanted, whenever I felt like it. This usually consisted of paint-by-number sets, TV, and tracing from the folding tables the free lines of a horse running amongst gold stars. My aunt would bring me onionskin paper from her job on Wall Street. Any one of these things would hold my attention for untold hours. No one called me out to play. No one called at all. There was no place to play except the little parks the adults never even thought of taking me to. *"I'm busy," "Laura, go do something"* was my middle name. "But I want you to do something with me" stopped with "Will you shut up?"

Mostly my grandfather (Alphonse, aka Al or BoBo) and occasionally my father (Leo, aka Daddy) would hold vigil all day or night downstairs in the funeral home when there was a wake. *"We have business; we'll be downstairs,"* or *"I'll be downstairs,"* were their middle names.

At the small office with no door, there was a wall at a right angle with a space wide enough to walk through. If you were tall enough, you could see over it, and even rest your arms on top and across it as people from the wake meandered around, looking for conversation unrelated to the dead person two rooms back. My father and grandfather would periodically invite family members from the wakes up for coffee and cake: the ones who said, "I'll go crazy if I have to spend another minute down there." They were forced to out of protocol.

All day long, until everyone went to bed, there was either a fresh pot of coffee on the stove or one still hot. Washing the coffeepot was the last action taken at night. The kitchen was infused with the smell of 8 O'Clock coffee, bought and ground fresh in front of your eyes at the local A&P, or espresso with anisette and a twist of lemon rind dropped into the cup. To this day, the rich smell of espresso fills me and reminds me of the richness of Italian culture. I will always love the smell of it. *Mmm*. . . espresso and embalming fluid just do something for the soul.

The sugar bowl was constantly being refilled, and the square glass ashtrays were constantly emptied and washed. There were always pound cakes, sometimes angel food cakes, Entenmann's, and store-bought cookies. If one of our family members or close friends died, there would be bakery cookies. I especially liked the butter ones with chocolate sprinkles. Fresh fruit was always available. My grandfather would have it with some kind of Italian cheese after dinner, an old Italian rite. Personally, I didn't like the smell or taste of any of the cheeses except mozzarella.

The pervasive smell of embalming fluid and death was just a part of daily life. Could you imagine saying this to a young friend: "You know, I really don't like smelling death and embalming fluid all summer, do you?" Watching them gag while saying, "Uh, gotta go" was not what my young mind wanted to see or hear.

Grandpa was about six feet tall, rotund, and bald on top, except for a few hairs that refused to leave and a horseshoe of whitish-grey hair. His smile put sunshine in my heart. He was always in black pants and a white shirt. A black jacket and tie would come on and off as needed. "Laura, go get Grandpa his knife" meant someone forgot to put it out for the fruit and cheese. He called me Speedy Gonzalez or "as skinny as a pipe" in Italian. I couldn't spell it if I tried.

Grandpa had lopped off the tip of his middle finger one winter day while adjusting something in his car's engine. The fan cut it off. He wasn't even aware it had happened. "It was so cold, I didn't feel it," he said. "Someone told me I was bleeding." It healed over nicely, thank God. It didn't look grotesque, and I knew it caused him no further pain.

He always held a Di Nobili Italian cigar of varying length between his index finger and that stumpy finger. I realized from the expression of satisfaction on his face when he would hold up those two fingers with the cigar in between that he was probably saying something I was not allowed to repeat. It always made me laugh. It made him look so impish, but those cigars stunk like hell. In the movie *Anatomy of a Murder*, Jimmy Stewart smokes them, and they are referred to as "stink weeds." Believe me, that doesn't come close, but they will always remind me of Grandpa.

The best memories involving those cigars were him picking me up from school in Mill Basin and smoking them for the half-hour to forty-five-minute trip back to his house. Then I would run up the two flights of stairs as fast as I could, head right for the bathroom, barf, sit for five minutes to stop my head from spinning, and have two bowls of pasta Faggioli. A ritual I wish had never been.

Grandpa would take me with him to buy them at the Te-Amo cigar store on the corner of Court Street. "Come on, Laura, let's go for a walk" was music to my ears. I could at least skip along or run up ahead of him. Fresh car exhaust was always good for the lungs. There would be pleasant conversation between my gramps and the guy behind the counter, like they were happy to see each other again.

My cousin Marie, my Aunt Camy's only daughter, was twelve years older than me. She was a young adult, doing young adult things I couldn't relate to at the time, except the music she liked to play on the radio.

My eldest sister Rita was eight years older than me, and would usually be off reading somewhere. "Hey, Rita, where are you?" I'd call. When there was no response, she was reading. She didn't have to say "*Leave me alone.*" Or, when there were no funerals, she would be sitting in Grandpa's office downstairs going through piles of pennies. She could trade a valuable one for silver at Mr. Rahey's candy store across the street. She would do this for hours and let me help too.

My sister Joanne was four years older than me, always off on her own somewhere, never to be found. I would have to hunt for her to see what she was doing. She rarely appreciated it if I found her. One day, I discovered where she went. She was exploring in the basement under the funeral home. She loved it. It was pretty much a guarantee there would be no way in hell I would ever follow her there. Apparently, that was where all the Christmas decorations and other household stuff was stored. I just wasn't taking any chances that something had been stored there by mistake. She would just say, "Get outta here." Joanne didn't like me. She had been the baby of the family once, and Aunt Camy's favorite, until I came along. She was still Aunt Camy's favorite, but no longer was the baby, the youngest. She held a serious resentment her entire life for that one. Joanne didn't get over things easily. Sometimes, nobody seemed to get over things easily.

I recall one particular day, when a widow had come upstairs for a break with my father for coffee and cake. The suffocating smell, the dim lights, and hour after hour of sitting there in front of the corpse had gotten to her. Of course, my grandmother was there as well as my mother. I remember I smiled at her as she entered the kitchen, then went under the table. I was small enough to be considered adorable (those days are certainly gone!). She was an elderly woman in a black dress, black shoes, and black stockings. I vaguely remember black hair; it might have been some kind of hat. She was so filled with grief, it seemed an effort for her to raise her eyes; I could hear it in her voice. Of course, some pleasantries were spoken around the thank-yous and you're welcomes. After a little time had passed and everyone settled down, I was given a cookie under the table. My dad said, "Relax," in a tone of voice that meant "you're among friends."

"My husband," she said. "He just lay there in the hospital bed, not wanting to leave or stay. He was in so much pain. We were just waiting."

My father was smoking a cigarette. "Did the doctor come?"

I could sense her head nodding before she said yes, because it sounded as if it were too difficult to say.

Then my father asked, "He gave him a little extra painkiller?"

Silence. She must have been crying, because I heard a sound of relief and deep sorrow.

Then I realized what my father was saying. In those days, the doctor decided when you would die if your pain was too great and your time too short. I learned on the spot what a lingering death was. How compassionate the doctor seemed to me, and how natural the unnatural.

There were other ways to administer compassion. Today, I know it is called euthanasia. I also know about telling a loved one it was okay if they passed. They would be all right, and they would find their rest, not to worry. I also know about palliative care.

I don't recall anyone at the kitchen table ever talking about a dying person being told they were dying! Even my grandfather wasn't told he was dying from leukemia. It seemed harder to let go then. Neither the words nor the spirit of the words were spoken. Maybe only the doctor had that ability. If they were spoken by the family, I doubt those suffering people would have been at our table.

There were the stories about abortions performed in hospitals, very hush-hush. They seemed to have been done out of compassion. That came up in conversations not about the dead person downstairs, but about people's family members. After people felt safe talking about death, all kinds of stuff would come out. These experiences still haunt me. I am better able to accept life on life's terms, but sometimes, things are just too big for various reasons. I don't approve or disapprove.

Since I never spoke to anyone about these matters, I still just ponder them. I'm good with that. Especially since I really don't find it particularly easy to see things as completely right or wrong. I learned early on that everyone is unique with unique circumstances, and death always comes with a loss. I was never really any good at absolutes, and I am still not that great at loss. A friend of mine recently said, "Death is written in the fine print of the contract." Tell me something . . . who really reads that stuff, anyway?

Wait a minute. I remember the first time I found it really easy to let go. I had an uncle Jimmy, who everyone in the family loved and thought was so funny. I couldn't stand him. He loved to torture me for fun. He was the guy who ran the cigarettes. It would be 7 a.m. on a Sunday morning. The dreaded school day would be looming closer, homework still unfinished. Packing up and the drive back home to Mill Basin loomed, along with the chances of not watching *Bonanza*. Then: "WAKE UP! THE DAY IS ALMOST OVER! WHAT ARE YOU STILL DOING IN BED!" He would bang the inside of a metal pot with a metal spoon in my ear.

I started to hate him more and more. Once, the boiler blew at the new funeral home and flew my father across the room. The skin on his face just hung off. After he came home from the hospital, you would never have known it happened, but I was devastated. I was still too young, according to hospital rules, to go see him. My mother let me make him a child-sized cake. They had them in those days—little cake pans. I was so proud. Then Uncle Jimmy came over and saw it. He grabbed it and said, "Look, there is a hair on it!" and proceeded to put it under the running faucet. My mom jumped up and grabbed the cake from him, saying, "It's okay, Laura," but I never saw the cake again. I just hated him.

Many years later, he died on Christmas morning. To this day, I want to put on my red shoes and dance on his grave. I still haven't received a better Christmas gift in my life! I wonder if he accepts the irony of that and laughs. I certainly do.

Mother Angelica, who created the Catholic Broadcasting Network, said, "I am not a recovering Catholic; I am a recovering Italian!!!" This is something we share in common.

Other things I heard from under the table were stories of dying family members talking to people who were already deceased. This was common. Hey, this was a time when men in their thirties were dropping like flies in Raid from heart attacks. People died at home, or from natural causes, more often—a lot more often then. It was not unusual for people to speak to the dead. It was just as accepted as eating cannoli on a holiday.

On these occasions, and if I had been there a while, as long as I avoided everyone else's feet, I could lean on my mom's legs, and sometimes she would stroke my hair. Looking back on this, I can see that I always hounded my mom. If I was treated like one, that, too, was natural, I guess.

A voice from the table would say, "We'd be there with him, just talking. Oh, you know Martha and Vinny? They sent flowers. That was nice of them, hadn't heard from them in a while, that was nice of them. Then Joe would start talking. 'What? What do you want, Joe?' I went over to him to hear him better. 'What, Joe? What do you want?' I said to him, but he was talking to his sister. He was talking to his sister Isabel. Isabel happened to have been dead for twenty years. 'Isabel, yes, have you . . . ? No. . .' We said nothing, just sat quietly with him. He was dying, we knew he was dying." And the crying would start again. I always thought, *What else did he say?* but it was really none of my business, and I never dared ask what they were talking about. I'd be heard from, and that would have been it—instant dead meat, banished from under the table.

It was something to think about. It was so cool, so extraordinary. I loved those stories. The person would be in bed, talking to their mother who wasn't there, or to someone nobody could see, but had known. Then they would start talking about that person.

"Remember how she was with her?"

"Oh, yeah."

There would be more than one family member at the table at a time, often two. It was definitely a different time. Funerals were on the last legs of coming out of people's actual parlors. We were just a funeral parlor. People had been embalmed in their homes not too long before.

When my father had to drive a long way to pick up a corpse, he would take us kids along. I remember my mother saying, "Take them, Leo, they will help you to stay awake." (Dad was working three jobs.) It was always a happy occasion. It was a new adventure to see something different, and that didn't mean dead bodies; it meant different scenery. It was always at night.

Once, after what seemed like hours of driving, we finally arrived. My dad got out and said, "Stay in the car. There is someone who is going to meet me inside and let me in. It shouldn't take too long." He went up to the door and rang the bell; no one answered. I was watching him. He rang the doorbell again, and waited a little while longer. No answer. He walked back and stood by the driver's-side door and lit a cigarette.

I was sitting in the back seat on the opposite side. I watched as an old lady opened the door to the house and looked out, with an expression that seemed to say, "Who are you? I don't know you. I'm not letting you in my house." She went back inside and shut the door.

My dad finished his cigarette and said, "I have to make a phone call. There was someone who was supposed to be here."

I said, "Dad, there is an old lady in there. She opened the door and went back inside."

"You sure?"

"Yeah, I saw her."

He went back to the house and rang the bell again. No answer.

"Laura, are you sure you saw someone?"

I started getting annoyed that he had asked me again. "Yeah, I saw her!"

"Well," he said, "she's not answering. I have to make a phone call."

In those days, there were no cell phones. You had to go find a phone booth. Usually, a gas station would have one, like air on tap to fill your bike tires with.

We drove for a little while, pretty much in the dark. It was in the country. Who knows—it might have been Jersey.

Once my dad found a phone, I heard him say, "My daughter said she saw someone in there . . . I'm sure." Then, "Okay." He got back into the car and announced, "He's late. He's going to meet us there."

We pulled back up in front of the house. Dad lit another cigarette and smoked it. The guy showed up. A little time passed, and they rolled out the body of someone in that famous black leather body bag with the zipper on top. I thought it was such good leather, it was a shame to use it on dead people. I would have liked to have had something made of it. Oh well, what could you do?

My father talked to the guy for a little while, I think about the arrangements or something. Back into the car he got. The corpse was secure, and the back door to the station wagon was locked. Everyone was accounted for. We were on our way home.

I waited for someone to bring up the fact that I had seen the old lady. Instead, nobody said a word about it, as if I saw that kind of thing every day: a ghost, the spirit of an old lady with an attitude. I couldn't believe it. They actually treated it as if it were not something really strange. My dad just shrugged his shoulders.

I had seen her as plain as day. She was pissed; she wasn't going to let my dad in, and didn't know him. But no one in my family ever brought it up.

Meanwhile, I was wondering if it was her in the back of the station wagon. If it was, she was being real quiet. Didn't say another word with a look, and if she did, I couldn't see it. Guess she had to behave herself and be dead. It was a consensus. "*Go ahead, lady, play dead,*" I thought. "*I'm glad that when we get back, I won't have to see you again and make it look like I'm the one who is strange to my friends.*"

Yeah, I wanted to go home and get back under my fort. It wasn't because I was scared of the ghost or spirit, whatever you wanted to call it. It was because my entire family was strange. They thought there was nothing unusual about me seeing that! How could I share something like with my schoolmates? No wonder I was scared of other kids. I didn't want to know their reaction if I spoke to them about it, or how strange I thought my family was. I developed a quietness—out of protection, and, quite honestly, out of curiosity. Aunt Camy and my father always said, "Think. Learn and think." Later on, I heard, "Listen to your gut."

I was given a mechanical squirrel for Christmas once. I loved that thing. It felt like it had real squirrel hair and a real squirrel tail. It would go into a wall then run down along it or turn around. I loved it so much. I wasn't crazy about dolls—they were too stiff—but a stuffed toy animal couldn't be beat. The squirrel wasn't necessarily soft enough to squeeze, but it ran like a real squirrel. It had its own squirrel moves. Somehow, I seemed to be doing the same thing.

It wasn't just my grandparents' table I would sit under. I would sit under anybody's table if I could. I wasn't picky. I thought it was always the best seat in the house. Dining room tables worked, too. Wedding tables worked, but not that often. I liked to dance, so I went looking for people who would dance with me. Worst of all, I would have to behave myself on these occasions.

Actually, it really wasn't so bad. Acting like a lady always caught my interest. The women in my family were all beautiful, and each one had their own individual gifts: talent, intelligence, inner strength, or all three. All had inner beauty that I thought made their outer beauty a mere reflection of who they were. I really did love every one of them.

Aunt Camy, however, scared me. She was such a strong woman, and always had her eye on me, but didn't smile. She was dead serious with me. Aunt Camy had strong nails, and I hated it when she would wash my hair in the kitchen sink—it hurt. She scrubbed my scalp with those nails. After a few *yeows* on my part and an "oh stop, you want your scalp clean," if I said, "No, I don't," I knew I would be banned to the closet, biting my own tail like that fox fur she had.

Yet I couldn't help but admire her. She was no one's fool, and traveled the world. She really wasn't what you would call a gentlewoman. Let's put it this way: it was easier to be under the table when she was around, and be quiet. She knew I was listening.

Aunt Camy was the one who cultured me, saw what I was interested in, and figured out what was best for me, what would bring me to fruition as a person. And she could cook. Bottom line—she was the one who allowed me to sit under the table. At the time, death was not a topic of discussion for children. Children were not even brought to wakes.

Aunt Camy may have been scary, but she was the woman I respected most in my life, and I wouldn't have minded one bit if I turned out like her. She was very honest, well-traveled, beautifully spiritual, religious, and very intelligent. When it came down to it, I admired and loved her the most out of all the adults. She made it okay to trust reality and be a strong woman myself. I've been blessed to live among the living and the dead, even surviving Aunt Camy with joy and laughter. It was a great victory, but the battle was brutal.

CHAPTER 2

How I First Learned about Culture Two Floors above People Being Preserved

As an italian whose life revolved around good food, I was taught simply, "The way you get to know someone who is not of your own culture is to sit down and eat with them over their food and good conversation." Thank you, Aunt Camy. Hey, she brought home wooden shoes from Holland—and it took me years to visualize someone needing and wearing wooden shoes, even though I knew about the windmills. Who was I to question her?

When I came across something unrecognizable on my plate, if I said, "I don't like that," I would get a chorus from the adults: "How do you know you don't like it? You haven't tried it, not even once. You have to try it at least once!" Dad said it in a matter-of-fact way, and Mom said it with a smile. Aunt Camy didn't have a smile on her face as she said, "You live in the world, and you are still small. Are you going to stay that way for the rest of your life?" She still had that fox in her closet, and she wore it. And there were dead people downstairs. Yikes!!! How could anyone stand up against all that and come out alive? I was allowed not to like something, but only if it had been tasted first—even if I took a very small taste. To the chagrin of my family, the foods I had the most problem with were Italian.

So that was how I avoided remaining small for the rest of my life. Rita couldn't have cared less. All she ate was chocolate milk, pizza, macaroni with chicken or meat gravy, and rib eye steak. Anything else really didn't work for her. Aunt Camy and Rita didn't have the best relationship in the world.

Even on Thanksgiving, dirty looks passed between Rita and Aunt Camy. They both knew what was coming: a huge tray of lasagna, a large bowl of Italian meat, sausage, meatballs, *braciole* ad infinitum in gravy, a dish of grated parmesan cheese, a capon, a big crusty loaf of Italian bread, and a bottle of Chianti on the table in front of Grandpa. A full Italian meal filled the table. A turkey in the middle looked out of place with a bowl of sickly-looking canned cranberry sauce.

On this particular holiday, there would be a show-down between my father and Rita. She hated turkey. "Rita. I don't care if you like it or not, you are going to have some, or you're leaving the table right now. Do you hear me?" That meant she would be banished from all foods for the rest of the day if she didn't do what he said. He insisted every year that she had to take at least a bite of turkey. All the children had to. We didn't mind it—just Rita. She swallowed that piece like it was a rock. Then she would smile and say, "Are you happy, Dad?" He would give her a look of stern satisfaction. She would gag, and I would feel badly but still laugh—not loudly enough for my father to hear, though. Rita would look at me and give a crooked smile, because she still had a bit in her mouth. Afterward, she stuck out her tongue, trying to get rid of the taste. Her victory of eating one bite of turkey for another year was hysterical.

Fear of my own family, death held over my head, and curiosity all molded me, with one caveat: there were foods I had to develop a taste for. I found scotch to be one of those things. But no way in hell was I eating any animal's brain.

As a child, I was given the opportunity to become very familiar with Middle Eastern people and their food. It is still the food I enjoy most. Mr. Rahey and his candy store were right across the street. He also sold newspapers. He was Syrian, tall and very thin; he worked constantly, and had a greyish color about him. He looked like he was giving his very life to support his family, with the possibility of dying too soon. He was frail. I never remember his store being closed. I know he wasn't open all night, but I also remember my dad being able to get a newspaper from him late at night. "I am going across the street to pick up the paper—I want to see the baseball scores," he said so many times it was burned into my brain. Grandpa would say, "I got the news this morning."

"Okay, Pop," was always my dad's response.

Mr. Rahey was a quiet, gentle family man, but if you finally got him to lose his temper, nobody would want to be around—time to head for the hills. I remember watching him when he talked with my dad. When they spoke, he always wore a look of genuine concern on his face, and was interested in their conversation. You could tell he cared about what they were discussing, and about my father. He was never without a ready smile for me.

Of course, my sole purpose in life when it came to his store was to chisel a nickel from my dad or grandfather for a Devil Dog—two chocolate sweet cakes with a chemical cream in between. Almost every day, I would go there as faithfully as the men in my family. "Here you go, Laura," Mr. Rahey would say if there was change. I think he smiled because of the look of victory on my face every time. I remember his smile. It was as if his heart rose up from somewhere in his hardworking daily life. He would give me a nod of acknowledgment with a warmth I can still feel. I still love the darn things, and feel victorious when I choose to buy a small box of them in the local grocery store. Whenever I do this, or even see Devil Dogs, I feel a warm, special smile. I can't help it.

Mr. Rahey was a good man. I knew that well enough. He was never out of Devil Dogs for me, and never without a smile, even if it was a small one. Grandpa knew it, and I think he just got a kick out of it.

I don't remember if it was Christmas or New Year's, but the Christmas tree was up. The atmosphere in the house was really good. This one special year, Mr. Rahey sent his daughter over to dance. All I knew was that he loved her so very much, and was so proud of her. His son was a friend of the family, too; he liked Joanne. Mr. Rahey would actually get brighter around her. He would stand up straighter, and light up when it came to his daughter . . . as proud of her as any father possibly could be. He had good reason, too. God knows where I was in the house at the time, because I didn't see her show up. I simply heard my mom saying, "Laura, Laura! Mr. Rahey's daughter is here, and she is going to belly dance for us." WOW! I don't think I ever ran as fast again, just so I could sit right in front of her on the floor.

I had seen belly-dancing clothes on the mannequins in the Middle Eastern stores on Atlantic Avenue. I took that five-minute walk practically every day. Now I wanted to see what they looked like when they were moving, not just still on some plastic woman. They sparkled with intricacies that only a person who understood real beauty could sew. And there she was, standing by the Christmas tree. It took my breath away. She was in the most beautiful belly-dancing outfit I had ever seen. She was so alive. In her hair was a piece of deep red velvet that fit the top of her head perfectly. Its material was sparkling. It had substance, and it held a veil that was longer than her long black hair. She had a face that seemed to have been transported from somewhere else. This was no Tarantella, that's for sure—or Bunny Hop, for that matter, or Polka, which I loved to dance more than anything. I don't remember if music was actually playing, except for those gold finger cymbals. If there was music, I didn't hear it that night. I heard Middle Eastern music all the time from the stores that played it so passersby could hear. You could tell they were songs of unrequited love, life, joy, and sorrow. I didn't have to understand the words; the music and heartfelt singing voice, whether male or female, said it all.

Her breasts and hips were covered and outlined in gold thread, embroidered on what looked like deep red velvet that changed shades when light was cast on it. It had what I thought were jewels sewed in amongst the sequins, and beads that sparkled with every movement she made. Mr. Rahey's daughter filled the room with energy and light I had never seen before. She was more beautiful even than the Christmas tree, full of life and light that danced and darted. Her belly was as bare as her legs and feet. Only veils covered them, part of the bejeweled deep red velvet and low gold low band across her hips—and it didn't do a very good job, at that.

Unlike the Spanish dancer, who creates and commands power on the spot and then succumbs to it with her castanets, Mr. Rahey's daughter held gold finger cymbals that didn't command power—they summoned it. Their sound changed the vibration of what seemed like the entire universe to me. The power of the heavens and the ether itself were captured and cupped in her hands. Then that same power became liquid that swam through her body, with a heart that beat music. Every movement of her arms, and the muscles in her abdomen, legs, and feet spoke. She spoke power and control, and the immense beauty of the creation of life and how it had begun. It started with the light sound of a cymbal made from the glint of metal of the earth, then became fluid and moved into solid ground with a life of its own. I had no idea a human body could talk like that.

Her big brown eyes and smile shone, and little colored lights and veils shimmered, and her supple skin and soft, strong muscles rolled up and down, back and forth, and side to side. With a step forward on the ball of her foot, there was a power in her hips that could move anything out of her way. Then I saw there was a jewel in her belly button! I said to myself, *she has a ruby in her bellybutton! We have innies and outies, but she has a ruby!* I know now it was not real, but then I believed it was. I couldn't take my eyes off it! I saw nothing else after that. My eyes finally traveled up above the ruby. Her bellybutton came up to a fine, perfect point that became the finest line of soft, dark hair. It was as if it pointed to the power of heaven. It was perfect. At the other end of this bejeweled bellybutton was the same thing, only it came down to a point with a line of dark hair that grew darker and wider. That point in her belly button pointed to the center of the earth. To this day, I have never seen anything more beautiful. It was exquisite.

I didn't know the word for it then, but I do now. Asymmetry. The asymmetry of her body was defined perfectly by this fine line of hair. It made the entire world fit perfectly: a mirror image of something that is not the same. It said one thing: the power behind the dance was life, it was creativity. She was free to move any way she wanted. With her movements, she was free to say anything she wanted to say. It was rapture.

I still see the veil covering her hair, the glint of light off her breasts, and that sparkling ruby in the center of the most beautiful belly button, used as a means to communicate life. I remained awestruck, even as I watched her leave with a smile on her face.

I was told later on, "Laura, do you know that belly dancing was originally danced only for women who were in the process of labor when giving birth?" I don't remember now who told me, but it captured my thoughts. This was so different from the idea of a dance for men's pleasure. It was only after I gave birth that I understood why it was only danced by women, for women. Sex and creativity create a life of their own. Giving birth while listening to these glinting cymbals, the power and strength and the music through a heartbeat with the rhythmic rolling of the belly, can bring forth the rapture of life itself. This was a dance of knowledge and empathy and communication, should the woman be close to death while giving birth. Any show of strength, empathy, rhythm, and beauty can save a life by giving one the will to live.

It is understandable why it is now danced for entertainment. Understanding its purpose, strength, and sacredness is a gift. I had a pretty good idea of this, even as a kid. We walked, talked, danced, and laughed the way we were used to. She danced a dance of life over death. For me, it was a Merry Christmas and Happy New Year, Laura! It's all alright. Life prevails, and it's beautiful.

There was a Syrian bakery—not Damascus or Sahadi's, which are still there to this day, but a very small one that was run by an older woman. Grandpa used to take me there. You had to go down three whitewashed steps. Never mind if it felt like you were taking your life in your hands while walking down those cracked, slightly broken steps. After you survived that, it was like walking into a different universe; it was walking into a bakery in Syria. The place was run by a woman who was excellent at her craft, and a natural at business. She was probably about five foot four, with grey and black hair—a little heavyset, maybe in her fifties. When you passed through the glass front door, you entered into this whitewashed underground room with a low ceiling, and not a great amount of space to work in, either. Three people in line at the store made it overcrowded. I loved the smell of the fresh, baking bread, the hot ovens, and those flat, round, deep golden-brown loaves. When they were still warm, they could be split carefully with a knife—even a butter knife—and the thin, disk-like bread would give way and separate, filled with little peaks and valleys.

The nutty smell of sesame seeds toasting filled you with a strong desire to have everything that was baking. The big white oven with the scorched-black top above the door had two men in white pants and white undershirts with white aprons tied around their waists feeding it raw dough and removing what we all shared in common: the stuff of life. They were always busy, either filling the long oven with bread or taking it out. "Just a little while, wait, they are coming out in a few minutes" was their rushed response when "Where are they?" was yelled out to them. The men were covered in flour from working with the dough on the dark wooden table in front of the oven. There was flour everywhere: on the walls, on the floor, and on them. It was a window into what my great-grandfather must have looked like as he worked more than a century earlier in the family's bakery.

There were two sizes of plastic bags, for small rings and large rings of Pita bread. Meanwhile, the smell of the fresh-baked bread started to infuse your pores. The smell of the raw flour became distinct, too. You saw the faces of the men waiting by the ovens, talking to each other. The woman behind the counter would recognize you, and when she did, her look pierced right through you as you became a part of her domain, her world. You became a part of her life, like the bread itself. She knew she was feeding you. "Which ones do you like best, which ones do you want today?" was her question to everyone who walked into the store. Or "Let me find the best one for you" as she rifled through the bags. She would always say that to Grandpa.

I paid attention to the tube-like loaves, because these were the ones I especially liked. They were on a low, beaten-up wooden bench behind us. When we got home, we would eat this thick bread, which always had a few burnt sesame seeds on it, by breaking the warm rings apart piece by piece, adding soft butter— either in the split made down the middle or on top— and then dunking it in hot coffee. I was allowed coffee at a young age, even though I was told, "It's going to stunt you." I loved the smell of it, and was willing to take the chance.

When it was your turn to put the bread on the counter from the bench and the baker from inside the glass case, there was always someone you had to smash up against to make room for them to come in. They would try to look at what was left on the shelves and bench; otherwise, they had to wait. People were lined up on those dangerous steps and on the sidewalk. Behind the counter, the woman looked work-worn. Even as a child, I could tell. She was so busy, she barely had time to chitchat, except if you took a breath in and gave a quick "How are you?" You'd get a shrug, along with a look that seemed to say, "How do I look like I am? I can barely breathe, I'm so busy, and am exhausted on top of it." Strangely, she looked like she was working herself to death out of love.

She was tough and gruff, and you knew she did not have an easy life, but she had something that spoke all languages, crossed all cultures and barriers, and could make perfect communion with anyone. It was the unspoken communication of love, care, and appreciation. She was a good woman. She loved her extended family, and showed it through her feeding and nourishment of them. It didn't matter where you came from, or how old or young you were. This is a universal blessing every part of the world shares. It is silent, and it speaks volumes in our lives. It's good women who care.

She aced it with her spinach pies. She made them with a dough that was not thick, but substantial enough to hold a mixture of fresh spinach, lemon juice, onions, fresh olive oil, and pine nuts. Each spinach pie was a small pocket with its edges folded in to make a triangle. It oozed a juice that could cure dehydration.

The taste, smell, and feel of it seemed to go on forever as you and it became one. It was completeness: bread, vegetable, flavor, olive oil, and warm juice, just crusty enough to nourish every part of you. When you paid her for these items, she would look you straight in the eye and give a nod of approval. When I remember her, I think, "If this is how a good woman cooks, I want to be fed by every one of them in the world."

The last time I saw her, I was thirty-two, and eight months pregnant with Rob. I had just been mugged. It was Christmas time; it happened about four or five doors away from her shop. I was so shaken, and felt so helpless and vulnerable, that I looked around for somewhere safe to be. I saw those cracked, white-washed, broken steps. I slowly walked down and went in. It was no longer crowded; there were no men baking. I was the only one there. It was just the woman and her daughter doing all the work. I sat on that wooden bench that no longer held the bags of bread. They gave me a glass of water, and let me sit until I stopped shaking and calmed down. There was nowhere else I wanted to be. The smell was still the same: it infused the place. Nothing of it had changed. As I calmed down, I looked across into the showcase and I saw it was filled with spinach pies waiting for children to come out of school. I left warm and safe and steady, but I just wanted to get home, and left as soon as I could thank them.

When you walked into Sahadi's or Damascus Bakery on Atlantic Avenue, you were no longer in Brooklyn, but transported to a market in the Middle East. Different varieties of nuts were kept in their burlap sacks or barrels, so their aromas and the sight of them were open, in full availability. High up behind them, shelves were filled with small, beautiful, exotic coffee pots with long handles. Now things are kept in square plexiglas boxes. The pastries were something I had to be dragged away from. Baklava: flaky pastry squares filled with crushed walnuts so sticky with rosewater-flavored honey. Bird's nests: a shredded crunchy phyllo pastry shaped like a bird's nest and filled with a crushed nut filling infused with butter, rosewater, and honey. There was a host of pastries I still can't pronounce the names of, but that didn't have any effect on their taste. Aunt Camy would buy me clear, crystalized rock candy sugar on a wooden stick with a little wooden ball on the end. I thought they were just made for children. They were beautiful. I later found out they are used to sweeten your tea or coffee. How ingenious, and tasteful; such a classy and delightful way to sweeten. I was, and still am, delighted by their beauty.

"Here, Laura." I knew she would get them to keep my mouth busy and me still, so I would stop being annoying and following my mother everywhere, watching over everyone's shoulder to see what they were doing and how. There was Turkish delight; *halvah* made from almond paste; and the little rectangular sesame-seed candy wrapped in clear plastic. The smell of Turkish coffee just topped it all off. The stores never ended, with all the varieties of enticing foods and smells. Middle Eastern music was played outside, and the windows were full of belly-dancing outfits, record albums, and things that sparkled. The music wasn't loud, but it couldn't be missed.

Many years later, in my fifties, I went back to Atlantic Avenue and stopped at Sahadi's and there was Mr. Sahadi—not the father, but the son, now a much older man. Everything was the same. All the varieties of foods were available, but now they were in endless rows of large, clear, square plastic containers. The big scoops were still there, used to fill plastic bags (not paper ones) with such richness and variety. There was Mr. Sahadi, still behind the cash register with a line of people waiting to pay for their wares.

I said, "Mr. Sahadi, how are you? Do you remember me? I'm Laura from Cobble Hills Funeral Home."

He looked at me as if he had to back into a different decade, a different time frame. "Al, your grandfather, yes, when my father ran the store! Oh, my God," he said to the young workers behind the counter with him who were probably his children, as if he expected to see what the place had looked like fifty years before. Then he came back and said, "Yes! Yes, I remember." A big smile ran across his face, and a laugh rose up from deep inside him. He was remembering something my grandfather said to him, I was sure. "How is everyone in the family?"

"My father passed away," I said, sharing the same sadness of a time gone forever, but so grateful we had experienced it. As I looked back over my shoulder, I said, "Do you still sell the bread in the rigs? I don't see them."

A small chorus rose up from in front of the counter. "No," they said as they remembered. "That was years ago, no more."

"No," Mr. Sahadi said, "we haven't made them in

such a long time," and his arm rose up as if to show the past that had been. Then he smiled.

I asked, "What about the old lady who had the bakery downstairs?"

"No, no more. She died, then her daughter took over and ran it herself for a while. But it was too much work all alone, so she closed it." He was grateful to think of her again, the both of them, though it was sad. We both felt this way, but were happy to share the blessing.

By this time, I had my few candies and a bag of spinach pies bought for old times' sake, but they did not look like the ones from the old lady's store, when you had to take your life in your hands going down those cracked, whitewashed, slightly broken steps. I said, "Thank you, Mr. Sahadi," and bowed my head in a gesture of respect. We were both so happy to have seen each other again. I picked up my brown paper bag and left the store, but as I walked out, I was a little girl and a grown woman at the same time.

I looked to my right and took a fresh breath of air, taking one last look at the memory of that tough, strong woman. No wallflower, that was for sure. There is a part of me that will always live in her little Syrian bakery. The part that saw a woman run a really good, successful business for the first time. The part that was nourished for decades, and allowed to feel safe when I needed it. I was transported in more ways than one into another life, a world away. A home is a home is a home. Mr. Sahadi still remembered my family. Especially my grandfather, and that had brought another big smile to both of us. He was remembered, and loved, too.

This made me remember that Dad had always made it home for dinner every night—even if he took a nap and went back to work on a night shift. "I'll be home at five," he'd say. Or sometimes at a different time, but not much later, because the six o'clock news was always on, and it was a priority. He always informed anyone who was in the kitchen of the news.

Every school weekend, the best time was after dinner, when the adults were having coffee or playing an Italian card game on Saturday evening until late at night, arguing and yelling at each other: "What's the matter with you? You should have played the ace of spades if you had it!" Then another game and laughing, speaking in Italian when they didn't want anyone to understand what they were saying, cursing under their breath at the cards or each other, more yelling, more laughing, then a loud "You deal." It was always fun watching them until someone lost a hand, and the yelling got louder than usual. That was my cue to beat it. At those times, the kitchen was thick with smoke: Grandpa with his black, skinny, knotty DiNobli cigars, Grandma with her Marlboro cigarettes, Aunt Camy with her unfiltered Camels, Dad with his Kent cigarettes, and Mom with asthma.

It would be quiet in the living room. The television would be put on as I went in to relax and settle down from the day. Aunt Camy's end table was on the left-hand side of the room, under one of two pictures of Degas's ballerinas. They were mesmerizing.

The living room called me to explore what was in it.

It was as if a genie slipped out and hooked me by the nose and drew me to open a drawer. There was always a chance I would get caught opening and eating the stuff Aunt Camy had filled it up with from the Middle Eastern stores. It's funny—I was actually never yelled at once by her. It took me years to figure out that it had all been bought for us to enjoy. Aunt Camy was really a lot nicer than I gave her credit for.

There was always a beautiful orange tart: dried apricot attached to paper that you peeled off by the piece. All you needed was a small piece for a big pucker. A big bag of Indian nuts. Little oblong or round ones that you had to crack with concentration. The shells could cut your tongue if you weren't careful; they had thin, hard brown shells that had to be gotten through to get to the nutty sweetness inside. There was a bag of seeds known as Bizet's, which were thick with salty pumpkin seeds. If you ate too many, your lips would feel like they were going to split from the white salt. Almonds, cashews, pistachios, and those nougats: chewy, sweet, egg-white pieces of heaven with either pistachios or almonds mixed in. And that sweet, delectable candy with a clearly distinguishable scent and a thin wafer that reminded me of the host from church—the piece of God I was given every week to sustain me to live a full life.

Today, when I find myself on Atlantic Avenue, these are the first things I look for and buy, even if it is just a few. I have to buy both the pistachio and almond ones, because I still can't make up my mind which I like more. I was deeply impacted by the neighborhood world then, and I loved every minute of it.

There was a Native American community near where I lived as well. They had built the Brooklyn and Manhattan Bridges with the help of a famous strength: their lack of fear of heights. In honor of them, I would like to leave you with one of their recipes. Ed, my son Robert's father who was born and bred in Canarsie, Brooklyn (a ten-minute drive from Mill Basin), told me, "There once was a Native Canarsie Indian who lived deep in the area, and still lived in a teepee. He was well known. The old people still remembered him as a neighbor, and still talked about him." I wondered how he survived the winters. For me, this struck a curious chord about the true reality of the people who lived in this, our neighborhood's environment, and what it had really been like in below-freezing winters and suffocating summers. It didn't sound easy, and it gave me much greater respect for Native Americans and their immense endurance.

The last Native Peoples in the area were pushed out of Canarsie into the Poospatuck Reservation near Patchogue, Long Island—which, according to the 2000 census, still had 271 members of the Canarsie Tribe living there. My cousins lived in Patchogue. Who knew?

Once, when my son Robert was young, the locals decided on a patch of land that would keep the Native heritage alive. They got in touch with the Mohawks from up north, and they were going to build a long house and live there. They got in touch the Mohawks, but not the Canarsie Tribe. The thought was that it would be educational, especially for the children. But the land was right off the Belt Parkway and they figured kids would run through the on-ramp traffic to get to it, and would likely end up as road pizza. So the idea was abandoned. They decided to have high school kids run a vegetable garden and give the food to the local senior centers instead.

One Thanksgiving, however, they did have a cultural event at which the Mohawks cooked traditional food and sold traditional jewelry. I believe they showed how to put up a tepee. They had food and stuff representing European heritage, too. Robert had bought me a pair of earings; the money had probably come from birthday gifts. That was so special. Too bad the land chosen was not safe—it would have been a perfect spot for it.

I didn't catch any of the recipes for traditional Native food—but one Thanksgiving, at the Plymouth Historical Society, I researched the foods that were actually at that original table, and decided to give an original Thanksgiving dinner. The Historical Society had an actual recipe book from that time, and I winged the rest. They had peas, so I made really good split pea soup. They had shellfish, and so did those, too. I had two six-foot-long tables filled with real traditional food, or as close to it as I could get without making my guests want to walk out by not recognizing anything on the table as a familiar Thanksgiving dinner.

There was a Native American recipe for Nasaump, made with ground corn, "bruised blueberries," berries, and crushed nuts. Here is a basic recipe for Nasaump, though there are variations.

1 cup stoneground flint cornmeal
⅓ cup small berries, preferably wild; or
    cultivated (strawberries or raspberries)
⅓ cup blueberries
2 tbsp. crushed walnuts
2 tbsp. crushed hazelnuts
2 tbsp. unsalted pumpkin seeds
3 cups water
¼ cup maple syrup

In a saucepan, combine all ingredients and bring to a boil over high heat, stirring constantly. Reduce heat to medium, and stir until it becomes the consistency of thick porridge, grits, or oatmeal. 10 minutes. Serve hot or wait until cold; slice and fry in butter.

It sounded really good, though the actual recipe book was not as clear cut. I am known for taking serious liberties with my cooking, and I made a really moist, very deep purple cornbread just filled with berries and all different kinds of crushed nuts that would have grown commonly in the area. I used maple syrup from Vermont to sweeten it, adding no sugar. It was so good, if you could get past the color. I didn't want to freak out my guests too much, but hey, they still had cornbread.

With the turkey, I figured everyone likes the legs so I made it with an additional two; there were four legs. My friend Phyllis introduced the turkey: "And here is Tom. He's from Chernobyl." Everybody loved all the food. Everything went except those two additional turkey legs and a lot of the purple cornbread, which I thoroughly enjoyed for days. It was a completely traditional, untraditional Thanksgiving dinner. It was great, except that Rita had passed away by then. She died at the age of forty. But this Brooklyn girl knew how to have a party—a weird little party that would have sent Rita over the top laughing, I am sure. Nonetheless, I hope you enjoy it.

CHAPTER 3

Oh! That's What We're Made Of

M<small>Y MOM WAS BORN IN MANHATTAN</small>, on the Lower East Side, in 1919. She had two siblings: my Uncle Benny and Aunt Cathy. My grandfather Peter was from Sicily, a tailor who married my grandmother Josephine in an arranged marriage. Grandma said to me, "He didn't want to be in the army and fight in Sicily. He didn't want to go to war. He was chosen for me because his sister had made the wedding dress of one of my relatives. The families had met, and knew each other, and my father thought it was a good match." Grandma was a seamstress, and their families knew each other. It was an arrangement made in heaven.

Grandma once told me, "Mothers-in-law and daughters-in-law come down from Heaven fighting." She never mentioned her mother-in-law, and when she did, that was all she said. She loved talking about her wedding, saying, "My father released white doves when we stood at the church doors after we were just married. The day after we were married, Peter took me by the corner of my dress and brought me back to my father. He said to him, 'The way you gave her to me yesterday is the same way I bring her back to you today.'"

I said, "Huh? Grandma?"

"His mustache stunk like tobacco smoke, and I couldn't even kiss him." She expressed the sentiment by holding her nose pinched tight between her thumb and index fingers. Either someone spoke to her about the minor detail, or got Peter to wash his mustache really well or stop smoking if he wanted any. All I know is she appeared to have won the argument—I could tell by that smile of hers. I think washing Grandpa's mustache won out, because she had three kids—whatever he had done worked. I never knew anyone who spoke like her except Aunt Camy.

"I adored my father, and he adored me. He loved me the most," Grandma declared. She never said a bad word about either of her parents. She always spoke of them with deep love and respect. "He was a baker; he was brought over to America by his uncle, who was also a baker." As far as I understood, at least one other family related to us lived in a building on Mott Street. She would say, "My uncles made wine in the house, the second floor." I don't know how much room that took up; she never described their home in detail. She would tell me, "I never remembered my father Chris without flour on his face, and it was even up his nostrils." Grandma described her own mother in this way: "She was as small as a China doll, and worked so hard." When she referred to her, it was as "my poor mother."

"One day when I was young," Grandma said, "my father took me in his horse-drawn truck to deliver bread here on Nostrand Avenue. It was still mostly farmland then. 'I want to be a farmer, and this is where I am going to live,' I informed him. 'Why?' he asked. 'It's as quiet as a graveyard.' I smiled at my father, and knew this was where I would live." Grandma kept her word.

My mom would also talk about her youth. "I remember the farms around the corner on Ralph Avenue. There were cows grazing there." By the time I had grown up, I saw a library, bagel store, and pizza store, but I still loved it. When I was little, there was nothing like that; there were none of those stores. I remember a bank and muddy, broken sidewalks. Yet it never lost the quiet somehow. There were fewer cars and a lot more homes, mostly attached, when I was growing up.

Especially in the backyard, time stood still. There was a lot of undeveloped land when I was young. It was so still and so quiet, you could almost hear the sun come up in the early morning. When the breeze blew, the leaves on the trees would rattle, then begin a roar of clapping, signaling that they and you were alive. The stars at night were like steady friends that would give a light show, with frequent shooting stars just waiting to be caught by sight on those oh-so-missed warm summer nights.

Grandma bought the first two-family home on our block. She eventually bought the attached two-family home. Each had a basement that was made into one floor. They lived there, and she rented out the rest of the apartments. Grandma paid $40,000 for each house. She told me all of this one day as she gazed out the window from her rocking chair, her feet up on a footstool. She wore a colorful floral dress, and she had long hair. It was white, but turned yellow-blonde near the back of her head. I knew that before she would talk to me, I would have to brush it until she was satisfied.

"I never knew a better tailor than Peter. There was a man once who had a hump on his back, and Peter made him look like he was standing as straight as anyone else. He never used a machine, and his stitches were perfectly straight and small. But he didn't have a head for business. He once opened a shop in Manhattan by the water, and all he managed to get out of it was tuberculosis. From then on, he had to spend a lot more time back home in Sicily, because the air was fresher and healthier there. The best thing about his tuberculosis was that we had to sleep in separate beds. I loved it. I felt like a girl again!" She said this with such relish, hugging herself. It was all I could do to hold back a laugh.

Grandma was the businesswoman in the family. She worked hard. "My brothers would come and wash the windows and do heavy work, and I would make their daughters a dress every time they came. All I would and could do was sew. There were chefs in the family. I learned how to cook like in a restaurant, but I never really had to do anything in the house. Grandpa

45

and I bought big, heavy bedroom furniture that was in the show window, and because some of it got sun-bleached that you really couldn't see, we got it really cheap. When we went to the opera, I would dress so nice. I would wear a rhinestone tiara, and it looked so real, nobody knew it wasn't diamonds."

Granted, she also had to burn all the furniture for warmth during the Depression so as not to lose the houses. At one time, more money than she had was needed to pay the mortgage. She pulled all her resources together and made aprons. "My children ironed them, then went through the neighborhood door to door, selling them. They cost a nickel, or a dime for a fancy one. I made the payment," she said confidently.

My favorite stories were about her father, Chris, whose real first name was Castrenzio. It took me weeks to find that out after she died, plus a trip to the Manhattan Hall of Records. I wanted to visit his grave and pay my respects. I knew she would appreciate it, and from all the stories about him, I loved him, too. To my surprise, there were already flowers on his grave—and it wasn't a holiday, either. The guy had never stopped being loved.

My great-grandpa ended up in America with a really funny story, and it only made me adore him more. Grandma told me this story over and over, and, like her, I never tired of it. "He was becoming a priest outside Palermo, and one night, while he was blowing out the candles in the church, there was a body being viewed for the funeral the next day. All of a sudden, the corpse in the casket woke up!"

I later came to find out that this was a common occurrence—so common that bells were put on caskets with strings attached. If the person came out of a coma they would ring the bell so as not to be buried alive.

"Well, he got so scared, he ran out of the chapel so fast, he almost flew. He ran, got a gun, threw his robes over a fence, and shot them." I figured the experience had kind of killed his desire to become a priest. "His uncle was getting married up north, so he went there," she added between sips of the tea she had told me to make her. "Eventually, the cops and priests from the congregation came to the family to find out if they had any information as to what happened to him." He met my great-grandmother at the wedding. The rest is history.

My mother said, "He really left because he just wanted to have sex." (He had nine living children. One had died.) That might have been plausible if it hadn't happened that one day, while vacuuming the funeral home, my mom hit a gurney with a corpse on it so hard the guy's arm fell off it. She ran so fast, she nearly "flew," and never vacuumed the funeral home again. So much for her sex theory.

I thought my great-grandfather was the best. Grandma told me a story about when the Black Hand, the Mafia straight out of Sicily, would steal children and ransom them. "If the ransom was not paid, they would send back the child's finger or ear," Grandma said. "Because of the bakery, my brother was kidnapped. They told my father he had better not call the cops, or he would be killed. So my dad called the cops, and they set up the street like they weren't there."

Right then, Grandma would tell me to go make some lunch. Ooh, I wanted to kill her! Off I'd go, and heat up the creamy vegetable and chicken soup she loved. After we had eaten and cleaned up, she would brush her hair again. She would wrap it up in what was called a *rat* back then. You would put in a roll shape, and pin your hair around it. She could do it in a minute flat. When everything settled back down, again the story would continue.

"So, the cops dressed up like garbage men and lamplighters and regular people on the street. Then my dad and the man exchanged the money, and the cops came down on him." She used her hands to express what catching someone by the shoulders would look like. "The whole gang was arrested, and they found about thirty children in a basement being watched over by one woman."

I guess Chris bought a gun after that, because somehow, the story of her taking the gun and shooting shirts on the clotheslines as target practice became something she relished. She would hold up her hand as if she had a gun in it, look down the "barrel," and show me how she did it. I bet Chris had a time explaining that to the neighbors while paying for the shirts she shot. Grandma wasn't letting anyone kidnap her or harm her father after that. She was also good at skinning animals and killing chickens. She was the one who taught me how to make a good wood fire.

I first learned about human trafficking from her. "There was a street in Chinatown where if you were pretty, especially if you had light hair, and you walked down it alone, you were never seen again. I stayed away from there."

Her dad still had the priesthood in his heart, though he never took his final vows. He had a shrine in the bakery where the people in the neighborhood were welcome to come to pray and say their novenas. When I went to find out if we still had family in Sicily, I found out that his name had been changed at Ellis Island when he arrived. The person at the counter had changed it to Lo Monaco, or "the monk" in English. So much for that.

Grandma also told me, "He almost threw my sister in the bakery oven for cutting my hair off. She was jealous of how much my dad loved me, and how I had beautiful auburn hair that he loved, too." The guy was a riot. How could you not love him? Her stories made another time, a century before, absolutely real to me.

Once, my mother was in the hospital, and Grandma had to watch us. It was winter, and she made me wash my face in cold water before I went to school. I hated her for that. I was freezing. She said it was good for my skin. When I was twenty-one, I decided that as a birthday gift, I was going to Manhattan to get a professional facial. I paid $45.00. After I had washed my face in lukewarm water, they told me I needed to run an ice cube over my entire face every day because it was good for my skin—that it cleaned, then closed the pores. *Oy vey.* I didn't hate her after that, but I could have kicked myself in the ass.

Grandma would call me *stupido* sometimes. Her frustration would make me laugh. Later on, when

I wasn't laughing anymore, she would give me that smile of hers that I eventually came to love and appreciate. I had learned something that was actually very good for me. Her honesty, though, was a killer.

I couldn't leave you without a recipe Great-Grandpa Chris made every year in the bakery, and if you are not careful, your entire neighborhood will come to your house and eat it. We called it Grain Pie, but it is actually called *pastiera*. It's a pie that's made for breakfast on Easter Morning. It is proof you can die and go to heaven! It takes three days to make (don't get scared, it's really easy), from Maundy Thursday to Holy Saturday. It is made and sold throughout the year here in New York, however, if you want it. If it is around, it is eaten all day long no matter what day it is—it's that delicious. I am sure it would make Chris see the face of God more clearly, knowing you were nourished and happy with it.

PASTIERA

A 9-inch springform pan is needed.
Oven: 350°F

Ingredients (for making the grain):
½ cup wheat berries or pearl barley
1 cup milk
1-2 tbsp. butter
Zest of 1 lemon

For the ricotta mixture:
2 eggs + 2 yolks
1 ½ lbs. ricotta cheese
1 cup sugar (or more to taste)
1 tsp. vanilla extract
1 tsp. cinnamon
1 tbsp. orange blossom water OR zest of 1 orange
1 cup chopped candied fruit

For the shortcut pastry:
1 ⅔ cups flour
½ cup confectioner's sugar
1 cup unsalted butter
1 egg + 1 yolk
Zest of 1 lemon
Egg wash for brushing

1st Day: Make the Grain
Place the wheat berries or pearl barley, milk, butter, and lemon zest in saucepan over medium heat. Bring to a gentle boil for 10 minutes, or until it becomes like thick oatmeal. Transfer into a large bowl, allow to cool; cover, then refrigerate overnight.

2nd Day: Make the Pastry Dough
Place the flour and powdered sugar in a bowl. Chop the cold butter into small pieces and rub into the dry ingredients. When you get a mixture that resembles breadcrumbs, add the egg, egg yolk, and lemon zest.

Knead until the mixture comes together, but don't overdo it. Wrap in plastic wrap and let rest overnight in the refrigerator while you prepare the filling.

Make the Filling:
In a separate bowl, using a fork or electric mixer, beat the eggs, egg yolks, ricotta cheese, sugar, vanilla, cinnamon, and orange blossom water or zest of orange. It should be creamy with no lumps, but still liquid. Cover and let the mixture rest overnight in the refrigerator.

3rd Day:
Preheat oven to 350°F
Roll out ⅔ of the pastry dough and place in the greased 9″ diameter spring pan. Cut off any overhang and add to the remaining dough. Roll out the remaining pastry dough. With a pastry wheel (or knife, if you don't have one), cut long strips about an inch wide.

In a large bowl, fold the cooled grain mixture, rested ricotta mixture, and candied fruit together. Transfer into the springform pan. Trim the pastry to the level of the mixture.

Now add the lattice top. **It is very important that the criss-cross creates diamonds, not squares**. That is what makes it so beautiful. Press the lattice strips to the edge of the pastry very gently, as they will be floating delicately on top of the filling at this stage. Brush the lattice with some whole beaten egg and water to make it turn golden brown and shine.

Bake for 50 to 60 minutes. You are looking for a perfectly done, crisp pastry with a beautiful amber-brown top. Allow to cool completely inside the springform pan. Refrigerate overnight and let it rest, then remove the springform from the sides.

Some like to add powdered sugar on top; others like to leave it the color of amber.

When pastiera came out for breakfast on Easter Morning, Grandfather Bobo (I don't know what Great-grandpa Chris did) insisted that a little saucer be placed in the middle of the pie. A cut was made around the saucer, then the saucer was lifted off gently. This way, you cut civilized pieces, and when it was eaten all around, you still had the little pie in the center to slice like you would a regular pie. Pastiera is, hands down, my favorite breakfast. Of course, my Grandma Jenny, my dad's mom, insisted that I eat an egg with bread before I wolfed it down. Adults can be so annoying at times.

It was stuff like this that made up for living over the funeral home and getting my first biology lesson. That wasn't as sweet to digest, but it was still infinitely fascinating.

One day, tired of being around adults, I went downstairs to the ground level and sat at the top of the two steps that led to the men's room and the apartments. I had to have been around six. Sometimes, I needed to be alone by myself. Above these two steps was the second-floor landing, where the ladies' room was, along with the banister and spindles I could grab onto and swing from above the steps, once I was tall enough. I remember it was cool there. The front door was to my back, and the entrance into the funeral home was on my right. It was kind of a busy, dreamy place when no one was there. The air was fresher and cooler because of the draft from the door. I remember how alone I was feeling, with no kids my age to play with. Sitting there in front of me was the stretch of hallway that led to the back yard through the men's room. There was also an emergency exit from the side wall in the back of the funeral home, where the bodies were viewed.

The backyard was small and ugly, with cracked broken cement with weeds growing through it. There was a fence that led to the backyard of someone's house. To the right was a little sectioned-off area, not very wide, where my grandmother grew a spindly silver dollar plant that leaned up against a pretty, neglected wall. Yet that plant made up for all of it. Silver dollar plants are so pretty and unusual. They give off leaves that are oval, like fine cream or white parchment. In the center, between the parchment sheets, is where the small black seeds are held. So delicate, so pretty. But the yard was a nightmare. I never liked going into it. The only use it really got that I know of was during the summer when my cousin Marie would put up a lounge chair and lay in the sun to work on her tan.

On this particular day, I really hadn't noticed the back door was open until Miguel walked through it. I was surprised. I liked Miguel; he was a Puerto Rican guy from the neighborhood. He worked side by side with my dad, doing everything, it seemed. He had a daughter my age, my dad told me one day. He wasn't really a tall man, but he was thin, dark, and good-looking. You could just feel his warmth. Everyone liked him, too—a really nice guy. I didn't get to see him as often as my dad, and he mostly worked across the street, one building up from the new funeral home and the twelve apartments. Three floors. Six in the front and six in the back, with two central air shafts between them.

Well, Miguel had opened the door, and he was looking down. In his hands, he was holding a five-gallon water bottle filled with blood and fluid. His intention was to pour it down one of the toilet bowls. The health laws were beginning to be passed, and had become more stringent. Dad was putting in a fully-tiled operating room across the street that met all the requirements. Miguel looked up and saw me. I looked at him and what he had in his hands. My first thought was, "Oh, good." I would have a chance to see some of the embalming process. Dad never let me near an embalming procedure. Kids were rarely even brought to funerals at that time. In a shot, my whole brain lit up. That was blood in there. That was what we are made of. The whole human structure— muscles, bones, flesh, movement, all of it—fit like a puzzle. All the pieces fell into place.

I became hooked on science in that split second of recognition. The blood and fluid became pretty to me. Then Miguel saw that I was watching him. He didn't know what to do. He kind of did a little dance, making up his mind: should he go back into the room where they were working, or continue what he was doing? He didn't know where to turn first. I just laughed to myself. It was funny seeing him all confused like that. Then he realized I wasn't screaming and running away.

I had no problem with it; I was curious, and liked it. I knew I was smiling at him. He kind of did an "okay" smile back, and with a quick shrug of his shoulders, continued on with his work. There was a time frame to work under, and he knew I knew it. So, no fuss, no bother. I knew my dad would have said something, and I didn't want to hear it. I just went back upstairs. I don't know if Miguel ever even told him. Dad never said a word to me about it. Maybe he was biding his time. I don't know. It was then that I had made the huge transition into the first grade.

After some time had passed, Aunt Camy bought me a nurse doll, and watched what I did with it. I remember Mom had mentioned it to me. I didn't play with it for long, though; I didn't like dolls. I happened to think the uniforms were really cool, with the white hat and blue cape and all. The nurses had a purpose, and were disciplined in it. I liked the way it looked. I had zero desire to be a nurse, but was seriously curious about anatomy—until Rita bought me a book on the anatomy of a horse, and I nearly threw up. I loved horses, and she ruined it for me. I didn't want to know what they looked like inside; they were just too beautiful as they were. To me, their skeletal system was really ugly to look at. I knew this hadn't been her intention, because she was so happy and contented that she had bought me something I could really appreciate. If she only knew how much I disliked that book. It might have been obvious that I liked the way things worked . . . but not that much, and not with horses. Barf.

I was more curious about human anatomy. In my Catholic faith, the basis of it was that you live, die, and live again. What was that all about? How did that happen? Could anatomy be the first step in it? If so, how? That got my attention. I was already interested in science, and it fit hand in glove with my faith.

The big story about me was that when I was born, I was very sick. Projectile vomiting and diarrhea. If I survived the first six months, I would live. Mom told me how everyone, including family, the neighborhood, and the church, prayed for me. As it became obvious that I had survived it, I had a slew of crosses given to me as gifts. Hey, maybe that's where my curiosity started. Subjects like these were thought-provoking to me.

CHAPTER 4

So, This is Death?

I HAVE COME TO LEARN and observe that there are many forms of death: some good, some not so much.

I remember the first time I felt betrayed by my parents: when I had my tonsils taken out. I was put in my onesie and wrapped up in my favorite plaid blanket, and told we were going to visit a friend. It turned out to be the hospital. I was so ticked off at them, and so hurt. To make up for it, my dad bought me a kitten: Pixie. He was my first kitten, and I loved that cat so much. He eased the pain, along with cool drinks and eating ice cream and Play-Doh. Don't ask me why I craved eating Play-Doh, but I did.

At least that wasn't as bad as Rita and I hiding in the big bedroom closet eating Vicks VapoRub, which we found out was poisonous later on. Oh well. No harm done, I think . . . but this could be the reason I no longer like the taste of strong mint and grease.

Well, I made it to the first grade, and I was the third shortest in line. Mary Queen of Heaven was the name of the grammar school where I would remain for eight years. I had four nuns and four non-nuns as teachers. That was when it started. Aunt Camy sat me down one weekend and told me, "Laura, I promise you that I will give you a reward for every gold or silver star you earn." Her gentleness with me seemed rare, but it was certainly unforgettable. She bought me albums: some were narrated stories, some were songs, and some were only music. It was so nice of her. I felt like she would be tough on me if I got a green or blue star, and I was right. No reward. I got a nod and "That is very nice." I would walk away, saying to myself, "It's a star, a pretty blue star. Doesn't that count?" It *was* pretty, and I had earned it. It made me happy, and I was satisfied anyway. Eventually, I found out that if I earned enough of them, she would relent and give me a reward. I kept a very accurate account of these gifts.

I wasn't happy about going downtown so much anymore on weekends to be close to my dad. It was disruptive. Straight from school we left, and mostly, Grandpa drove us. I still get woozy just thinking about those rides and his DiNobli cigars. Five of us were in the car with Cleopatra, a dog the size of a Dalmatian, and Pixie the cat.

Next door to the new funeral home, which was almost finished by that time, was a fire house, and they had a Dalmatian named Queenie. Queenie was always having puppies. Well, once, when Queenie had her pups, they all were white with black spots except one. That was the one Dad brought home. He pulled her out from under his coat one night as he came home for dinner. We all started screaming at once, "A puppy, a puppy!" She was all black with three white spots: one on each of her two front paws, and one on her chest under her neck, between her shoulders. "Let me hold her," we all asked at the same time. My mom said, "She's so beautiful, Leo." After things calmed down and we had each had a chance to hold her a bit, it was time to name her. I remember this happened while she was eating. My mom said, "Let's call her Lady," but my dad said no, looking down at her from his seat at the table with a cigarette in his hand. "She is so black, and she shines like a diamond. She is too beautiful. Let's call her Cleopatra," he said. And so we did.

Eventually, we got another cat, and called him Caesar. This only occurred because one day, Pixie got hit by a car and died. It happened in front of our house, right as I was returning from school, I was told. A neighbor who saw it and was concerned that I would see him all bloodied and dead disposed of him somehow, and washed the blood off the street. That was such a kind thing to do. I don't remember who did it. I was so upset when Mom told me. I have always been highly sensitive, and that image would have burned into my soul. In my imagination, I saw what he looked like anyway, and the image got worse as I grew older, because I did see cats hit by cars. I rarely think of it any more. My poor cat—it feels as if I saw him lying in the street anyway. Imagination can be much worse than reality sometimes. I still get a pang if I think of the accident. That was the first time I realized what death was. Such a painful loss, and I knew I wouldn't be seeing him anymore. I remember looking out the window and crying. I was alone, but my dad saw me. He knelt next to me so he could talk to me at my height, and held my wrists. He explained so gently about death.

"Laura, I know it hurts, and that's all right; you loved him. Dying, Laura, is a part of life, and that doesn't mean it's a bad thing. It is a natural thing. It's okay if you hurt, but you also have to remember that the way God made it, Pixie will always remain in your heart and memory, and it can never stop you from loving him. That isn't such a bad thing, either, because that way, he will still be with you, and never have to die again. Come on, let's get away from the window."

Pixie will still be with me, I thought. I stopped crying, because Dad was so loving and so tender. I had never experienced anything like that before. I could hardly believe people were capable of being like that. It had a profound effect on me. Somewhere deep in my heart, I wanted to be that kind, too. He was so wonderful. I was comforted, so at peace with that kind of love. I still smile when I think about petting Pixie and picking him up.

Well, I got through my first year of school . . . barely. I loved horses. I used to carry little plastic ones in my pencil case, and play with them during class. My first-grade teacher was a Dominican nun. They are known for great education. All the nuns were Dominicans. Christmas came around, and Felix Amato's family donated the crèche (Nativity) for our classroom—the depiction of the birth of Christ. It was a little open barn with hay, with Mary on one side of the infant Jesus and Joseph on the other. Barn animals, cows and sheep, surrounded them, along with the angel and the three kings. Sister asked me, "Laura, would you like to put your horses in the Nativity?" My horses, there at the birth of Jesus? Oh, you bet. I said yes, and was humbled.

When we came back from Christmas vacation, it was time to take the Nativity scene down and give it back to Mr. and Mrs. Amato. I went to it, and my horses were gone! They were nowhere to be found. I remember Felix walking into the classroom, and meeting him. This is how the conversation went.

"You have my horses."

"No. What horses?"

"The ones I put in the Nativity, you took them when it was being packed up and you have them."

"No, I don't."

"Yes, you do, you stole my horses!"

"No, Laura, I didn't."

I was convinced he had stolen my horses, and nothing would convince me otherwise. I never forgot that Felix Amato stole my little plastic horses, and I held a resentment in my heart for him until I was in my forties—when one day, Mom and I were sitting at the kitchen table, having coffee or tea and talking. I don't remember why, or what we were talking about, but I brought up the time that Felix Amato had stolen my horses.

Mom looked at me and said, "He never stole your horses; the nun took them."

The first thing I blurted out was, "What? I have been blaming Felix all this time, and he never took them?" *Oh, no,* I said silently to myself. *Poor Felix. I have been blaming him all these years, and he never did anything to deserve it.* Then, with an attitude, because now I was getting angry that I had blamed Felix under false pretenses, I asked, "Why would she take my horses?"

"She told me she took them because she wanted you to understand that anything you adore more than God will be taken from you."

"What? What the fu—? What?"

Now I was angry that I had blamed Felix when there was no reason to. I was right that my horses had been stolen, but it had been done by someone I greatly respected and loved. I don't think I ever once saw her lose her temper while teaching a class of sixty children by herself. I couldn't believe what I was hearing. I was so angry, I couldn't even give thought to the belief that "things I adored more than God would be taken from me." I brushed this off as being just as ridiculous as the fact that she had taken my horses. The subject was dropped. It all made no sense to me.

The next time I talked to Felix on Facebook, I said, "Phil, I'm sorry I blamed you for taking the little plastic horses. You never did—plus you told me the truth, and never lied to me." He was cool about it. I didn't even know if he remembered it or not. Over thirty-five years had passed. In any case, I regretted it. He didn't deserve the negative energy I had directed at him all that time.

By the time I was in second grade, the new funeral home was being finished. There was a last-minute flurry of work being done. Vincent, the interior designer and painter of the casket room, was there. Dad had a mural painted on the wall on the right hand side as you walked in—a landscape. Vincent was at the apartment a lot for coffee and friendship. I remember one day, all of us were in the kitchen, and the three of us were ganging up on him.

"Vincent, can you sketch me?" Rita only had to say it once.

Then, Joanne: "Vincent, can you sketch me, too?"

Me: "Vincent, if you are going to sketch them, you're going to sketch me, too, right?"

He was very tall, with blonde hair and blue eyes. I remember thinking, "Does being tall make you an artist?" He was the only artist I knew.

Rita sat for him, and he drew her.

"Oh, it looks like her!" we said in chorus.

Joanne: "Okay, Vincent, my turn!!"

Joanne sat for Vincent, and he drew her.

"Oh, it looks like her!" came the chorus again.

Then, "Me, me, Vincent!!!"

By this time, I think Vincent was worn out. I climbed into the seat in front of him and smiled, then decided to put a serious look on my face. I looked into his blue eyes, which I thought were pretty—we all had brown eyes—and I smiled again. I probably fidgeted a bit, too. Then he stopped.

"Are you finished?" I asked with great anticipation.

"I can't seem to draw you; I can't capture you," he said.

I was devastated. "Why not?"

"Just can't."

I knew I couldn't keep it up, or my father might tell me to stop. That was the last thing I wanted. I never got a sketch of myself from Vincent, the first artist I ever met—but I think if I hadn't been happy with it, it might have been worse.

The architect had to sign off on everything, certifying that it was safe and built to code. So did the licensed electrician, Cappy, a skinny little Black guy who always was nursing a beer and nothing else. I think the guy was constantly crocked, but he was loved. He remained friends with my family for many, many years. He and his wife would come for dinner. Dad and Cappy would spend hours talking in the funeral home office. He would just come by to visit. Anytime anyone was near the funeral home, they would come and visit for coffee and a chat.

The architect, however, was a real character... the strangest man I have ever met. He dressed immaculately in a three-piece suit without a wrinkle, a pin holding his shirt collar together under his tie, a tie clasp, cuffs, and white shirt, stiff from being so starched; it was uncomfortable just looking at it. His vest was so fitted it looked like it had been sewn onto him. Shined shoes, a clean gold ring with a clean stone in it, manicured and clear-polished nails. There was nothing out of place anywhere, ever. I bet he wore suspenders to hold his socks up. There was never a hair out of place in his black, razor-sharp, parted-in-the-middle, plastered-to-his-scalp hairdo. I think if a hurricane hit this guy's head, a hair *couldn't* move out of place. He had black eyebrows and dark brown eyes that measured you when he looked at you. He was short and heavyset, hands always folded in front of him. Everything was measured about him: his steps, his breath, and even his thoughts. He was put together meticulously—so stiff, he could have been a walking architectural plan of what a mortician should look like. I stayed away from him as much as possible. He spooked me as a kid, and does so no less as an adult.

One day, years later at work, I came rushing into the office for whatever reason, and he was there in the lobby with my dad. I stopped dead in my tracks and said hello. He proceeded to lecture me about how the part in my hair was not razor sharp. "Look how messy that makes you look, and unprofessional, too. How can you come to work like that? Don't you have any pride in your appearance?" I looked at him, then at my dad, who seemed to nod in agreement. "Damn," I thought, *this guy is a real pain,* but I thanked him and mumbled something about being in a rush, and took off. Every time I ran a funeral and checked my makeup and hair before leaving, I looked at the part in my hair and mumbled something about what a pain that guy was.

When he died, my dad told me he'd said to him that when his apartment became available, I could move into it. I'll bet it was stunning, kept in absolutely perfect condition. The guy liked me, but he just creeped me out. Interestingly, my best friend later in life was an architect, and I admire architects greatly. And I like criticism if it is accurate, and not mean-spirited. Life is strange.

Finally, the new Cobble Hill Chapels, Inc. was open. It took up the whole corner, and both sides featured a grey-and-black marble front. It was a beautiful red-brick, four-story building with white window frames. There were double glass doors at the entrance to the foyer, and another set of double glass doors into the funeral home, which were always kept free of handprints. There were red carpets, red leather sofas, wooden end tables, and a water fountain that still provides the most delicious, ice-cold water. There were lamps on each table, and a statue of Moses—who looked like he had horns, but in reality, it was a depiction of flames.

When you walked in, the first thing that caught your eye was the large fountain. Water ran from a smaller shell into a larger one, and on the top of the fountain was a statue of St. Jude Thaddeus. He is always confused with Judas Iscariot, the one who betrayed Jesus. Jude means "bearer of joy," and Thaddeus means "generous and kind." St. Jude was thought to be a cousin of Jesus. He is the patron saint of desperate cases, and exhorts keeping your faith in the love of God. It was a beautiful fountain, and the sound of the gentle running water always drew my attention like a magnet. One day, I got my nickel from my grandfather to buy my Devil Dog, but was compelled to put it into the fountain. That was the one and only time I gave up my nickel. As a result, Dad was inspired to give whatever money had been dropped into the fountain to St. Jude's Hospital for children with leukemia. Now it is known as St. Jude's Research Hospital, where no parent pays for medical expenses, or has to pay for anything, for that matter—even food and lodging for the family. All medical advancements are shared with the world. When we opened, there was a big party, and I made it into the newspaper for the first time for giving up my nickel in the fountain and the inspiration this produced in my father. I was seven.

Well, now it was time to wait for the first funeral to christen the place, so to speak. Nothing. Weeks passed, and nothing happened. I was so anxious, I began to play funeral director. I think something was wrong with me from the beginning (Rita agreed.) My grandmother would call up the business phone, and I would answer it. My grandmother would say, "My husband died." My usual response was, "Oh, I am so sorry. I'll go get my daddy." Very professional, wouldn't you say? I really didn't want to be a funeral director; I wanted to play secretary, to be like my cousin Marie and Aunt Camy. They always looked so professional when they went to work on Wall Street. It was inspiring—but in my mind, it was like killing two birds with one stone. I could be in the middle of everything and act like the successful women in my family. You know, when you put so much of your life and your family's existence into opening a new business, it is a terrible feeling to wait for it to succeed. Life fell back into a routine.

We had many neighbors on the block in Mill Basin. The homes were all two-families and attached, except for two on our side of the street and one on the other. These were one-family homes with two floors. To our right was my Aunt Catherine and Uncle Johnny's house. They had three children: my cousin Rose, who was close to Rita's age; Dominic, who was close to Joanne's age; and Janet, who was close to my own. Grandma and Grandpa Peter lived on the first floor. Next to them were Mr. and Mrs. Vetucci. They had two boys, Mike and Paul. To our left were Mr. and Mrs. Manaco, Pete and Lena. Mrs. Manaco had her mother living downstairs, at first; then, when she died, her brother moved into that apartment. They also had three children.

Next to them lived Bobby and his wife Margie. Bobby was Irish, with blonde hair and bright blue eyes so alive, they always seemed to smile. He was a young man, very, very attractive, and he loved me. He had two boys, and wanted girls. My dad had three girls, and wanted boys. In his heart, my dad adopted his boys, and in Bobby's heart, he adopted me. Anytime I saw him after the age of four, I ran to him, and would stick to him like glue. He would pick me up, look me in the eye, and say, "You are so pretty" or "You are so cute," then put me down and hold my hand. I was in love with Bobby. I think I loved Bobby more than my dad. Of course, he never had to scold me for anything.

One day I remember particularly well came to pass before it was okay for little girls to wear pants. It was warm outside. I was in my little dress, and my dad and I went outdoors—him for a smoke on the stoop. Bobby was outside, too. I ran to Bobby, and he picked me up and sat me on his car between himself and my dad.

You know what that means when a guy picks you up and sits you on his car don't you? Well, that was proof he loved me more than his wife. So, when Margie came over—she had really pretty red hair, I remember—I promptly said to her, "You can leave now, because I am going to marry Bobby."

She just looked at me, looked at her feet, looked back up at me, and asked, "Okay . . . now?"

I said, "No, later."

She said, "Oh, okay."

I was content. She didn't give me a fight.

Rita bought me the record "I Want to Be Bobby's Girl." I think I wore the thing out, the way I played it over and over. How my mother didn't just hand me over to Bobby and say, "Here, you take her," I will never know. My mother had the patience of a saint at times.

One day, in the kitchen at my grandparents' house over the funeral home, my mother said, "Laura, Daddy wants to see you downstairs." I didn't know why, but what the heck, if he wanted to see me, he wanted to see me. I went down the two flights of stairs and saw him in Grandpa's funeral home, which was now closed and no longer in use. I was surprised. There was Dad, standing next to a gurney with a corpse on it, in that really nice leather bag that had that nice strong zipper up the middle. Dad didn't say a word to me—he just looked at me. I ran to him, and we stood, one of us on each side of the gurney, looking at the corpse. I looked back at him, and jumped for joy! Now Cobble Hill Chapels was open for business, and this time, the body was going across the street to the brand new funeral home. I was happy, so happy and proud that my dad had shown me the first corpse to go there.

This funeral would change everything. Boy, oh, boy, was I proud. We didn't say a word to each other, but my joy was obvious. Then, without a smile, he said, "Go upstairs." I didn't care that he had said so little to me; he had made me a part of the celebration. I flew up the stairs to tell my mother. Mom was sitting at the kitchen table with her back to that beautiful tiled wall, a cup of coffee in front of her. I ran around the other side and climbed into the chair across from her. With glee, I said, "Mom! We got our first funeral!" She gave me a little smile, and said, "I know. It's Bobby." He was thirty-five, and had died of a heart attack.

Something dropped out of me. With the realization of what she had said, all of a sudden, in the blink of an eye, I felt empty and numb inside. There was this emptiness in me that only Bobby could fill. I went back downstairs; I didn't want to be with anyone but Bobby, but Dad had already left. So I sat at the top of the steps, with the front door to my back, and felt like I was hanging in two worlds. One had everything I knew, and nothing had changed; the other was empty, with no words. I felt so alone. I felt like Miguel in that moment: I didn't know where to turn, or what to do. No one could bring him back. I would never see him on the block again; he would never say anything to me again. Something inside me shut down and died with him.

I thought, *if this is what the funeral home across the street has brought, I want no part of it, ever.* It completely lost its charm for me. How does one celebrate the success of a business and simultaneously die inside because of it? Something in me changed—the way

I even thought of corpses from that day on. They deserved tremendous care. This was a human being who had been miraculously made and miraculously loved by someone. I had become a part of every one of their stories and lives. I went upstairs, and never spoke of Bobby again. I couldn't. When Margie came over for coffee, she had been crying so much, there was no masking it. It was many years before I saw her laugh again.

From then on, someone named Bob or Bobby always played an important role in my life. My son's name is Robert. I could never call him Bobby. I call him Rob. Bobby really never left me, and neither has the joy. It has grown exponentially.

The nun was right. There were only two things I loved more than God: Rita and Bobby. Both were taken from me, but not by God. Patience and faith that somewhere, somehow, an unconditional love exists is not necessarily an easy thing in which to believe. Funny thing, though—a greater love has been given back to me in return.

So much for second grade. I passed everything, and made it into third grade. I was happy when it ended—no school for the whole summer, and I was growing up, too.

CHAPTER 5

Life as I Knew it Ended at Eight Years Old

THINGS BEGAN TO CHANGE after the new funeral home opened. Dad started to change. He started to become a little detached, but not in the usual busy way. Something was happening in the family. Things were changing. I remember a slow dread creeping up on me. I did not want to turn nine.

It was a typical New York summer heatwave. Go-to-the-beach-or-die kind of weather. 100 degrees, or even 101, was nothing unusual, with high humidity to boot. We had no air conditioners at that time. Very few people did. Only fans of different sizes: window-sized ones and table-sized ones.

Rita said, "Ma, I want to go to the beach." Going to the beach was just what you did in Brooklyn, especially in the summer. My mother wanted me out of her hair. There was nowhere else to go, and nothing to do. It was just too hot, and I'm sure she didn't want me suffering from the heat in the house, either. I waited for that magic moment again. "Rita, take Laura with you." It was like striking gold, hearing those words. When we were at my Grandfather Al's home, we went to Coney Island. When we were in Mill Basin, we went to Rockaway Beach. Either one worked fine for me. Then my mother added, "Rita, keep your eye on her; she's a fish." Rita's response was always the same: "Okay, Ma." I loved just being with Rita. She loved me, and maybe she wasn't so responsible, but she was the most fun to be with.

Packing for the beach started immediately. I had to get the right-sized beach bag, the right-sized sheet to lay on the sand.

"Double sheet," said Rita.

"Yeah," said Mom.

Then, the big decision: "What do you want to drink? And how do you want to carry it?" Rita wanted cold milk; I wanted lemonade. That meant two thermoses. The more you carried, the less you had to spend on drinks from that sweaty guy in the white clothes who carried a big silver cooler that kept things ice cold and yelled, "COLD DRINKS, COLD DRINKS," as he walked across the different sections of the beach. His price was higher than what you would pay anywhere else, but you always ended up looking for him and buying something anyway.

"Got the suntan lotion? Don't forget that."

Then, famously, my mother would always say, "And bring a hat!"

"Okay, Ma," we would both say together, then forget them anyway. Or, if we remembered them, the hats would always land at the bottom of the bag, filled up with sand and never used because they always blew off. They were a real pain—you would have to chase after them across the hot sand, loudly yelling, "OOCH, OUCH." I tried to run on the scorching sand and avoid touching it at the same time, putting the smallest possible surface area of my foot down until I was back on the protection of the sheet. Not using hats to start off with and just allowing them to fill up with the sand satisfied my mother, because it looked like they had been used. Unless you were with her . . . then there was no getting away with it. Otherwise, a towel over your head or face to protect it from a painful burn worked best.

"How many towels? And where are they?" I heard as I went to get my bathing suit.

You had to wear something over your bathing suit that wouldn't put you in agony from the sunburn and gritty sand that had to be endured on the way home. There was an art to this. You could start out with your bathing suit under your clothes—then it wasn't so embarrassing taking off your clothes in front of a thousand people. But that made it tough if you were not around the bathrooms to change *out* of your wet, sandy bathing suit and put underwear and clothes back on. If you were young, you could change on the beach while someone else held a towel around you. Once you got to a certain age, however, there was no recourse but to put your clothes on over your wet, sandy, burned skin (no matter how much suntan lotion you had put on). If you were a fish, Coppertone washed off, and you knew you were going back in the water again as soon as you started to get hot—which, during a New York summer, does not take long. It had to be thought-out: the smallest possible amount of clothes actually worn, but not so little you would get into trouble with the cops for not having sufficient clothing on over your bathing suit.

How things have changed. When Robert was around five, I took him to the beach. After a while, a woman put her blanket down next to us. It was no problem until Rob noticed she was lying topless. Robert positioned himself in such a way that he would not miss an inch of that view, and remained trans-fixed, jaw open. Even when the woman felt his stare, turned her head, opened her eyes, and watched him back, there was no shutting of his jaw or breaking of his focus. She smiled, just short of a laugh, and turned her face back to the sun. I almost had to put a towel over his head and carry him off to the shore to break his attention on something he had never seen on the beach before. I think what did the trick was when I said, just as intently, "Come on, Rob, let's go in the water." I happened to have given birth to a fish, too. I knew what would work.

No matter how much time passed, in every other way, the beach was timeless.

The next necessity was food. "What kind of sand-wiches do you want to eat?" Mom said. Rita and I agreed: "Bologna on white." It was a given that the dressing would end up being sand—Brooklyn's idea of fiber. Oh, yes, and ripe, deep purple, ice cold, sweet, juicy plums, sprinkled with enough sand, were always a great way to sandblast your teeth. Then, after you turned into a prune in the water and were forced to dry out, the question became: what to do? Rita was an avid reader, so it was easy for her: a book, or magazines, or both. Me? It all depended on how much I wanted to carry and not lose in my pail. I definitely needed a shovel, and it didn't need to match the pail. A variety of colors was good. The decision came down to this: did I want to carry the plastic forms, stars, fish, etc. to fill with wet sand and decorate the shore, or the area by my blanket? They were easy to lose, and were brought mostly when Mom was there, as she always agreed to be responsible for them. You could count on her.

Shoes? Flip-flops? Sandals? Another decision that had to be made. How hot would the sand be? This was learned only by experience, and depended on which would hold the least scorching sand. You would be going home with a shoe full of it, no matter how much you tapped out.

Off Rita and I would go for the walk to the subway just a few blocks away, all the while passing coolers and beach bags back and forth to each other. Then we would say a prayer to get a seat on the train, so we wouldn't have to be standing up, tossed from one side to the other—or holding onto a pole (or a stranger, if you couldn't reach the straps or bars overhead, which, of course, depended on your height). If there was no one in the train, you climbed onto the seat and made it to the other side of the speeding train hand over hand.

If our prayer was answered, two seats would be available next to each other. "Thank God" would be heard from both of us. We always had to have a plan if we got separated in the crowd, and that had to remain clear; otherwise, terror would strike. Rita's for losing me, and mine for being lost. What would Mom do to us if that happened? Each of us owned a wooden spoon with our name on it, but the iron spoon with the holes—the one used for Sunday dinner to take meat out of the pot of gravy—that was the one that would be smacked across our butts, and it had all of our names engraved in it. Whatever happened, NO GETTING LOST!!!!

It was the same with my son Robert—we had our plan, too. One day, he got lost in the crowd and went straight to the cops, just as our plan stated. Instead of going to the cops and following our plan, however, I ran around yelling out his name, crying and terrified until the cops found *me*. Then Robert asked, "What took you so long?" I think I was still shaking and crying, and I was so relieved. But never mind about that

Making it to our destination without getting lost was always a relief, and the closer we got to the beach, counting off the stops, the more the excitement would rise. We could finally put our stuff down, relax, and not be bounced around in a closed, crowded train with no air conditioning in a heatwave. If we wanted to talk, we had to yell at the top of our voices so we could be heard over the roar. Rita would say, "Next stop, make sure you have all your stuff." I would count everything, and return the statement with, "Got everything." Then the train would stop. We had about five or six seconds to get through the crowd leaving the train car, and again, we had to avoid getting lost or separated while carrying all our stuff, pushing through the crowd of people.

When we finally made it, it was like we had been shot out of a gun. We had some breathable space. Then it was just a matter of time to catch our breath, balance our stuff, and head to the scorching sand that almost blistered our feet—and water so ice cold, it would take us twenty minutes to stop shivering the minute we touched it. Then big smiles, relaxation, and a happy "the beach!"

That was the battle cry. We had to make it to a spot close enough to the water, but not so close that when the tide came in, we had to move everything farther back. We wanted to be near the lifeguard outlook for two reasons: safety, which was never given much importance, but we were happy they were there for someone else; and to be able to find our blanket and know our position so we didn't get lost. The tide, the waves, and the swimming could move us from our original entry point into the water. If we could see the lifeguard tower, we knew our blanket was somewhere around there. It was never a guarantee that whoever you went to the beach with would be on the blanket when you came back. It was understood there was just so much heat you could take before needing to cool off. A little bit of solitude was always welcome, too.

It could get so crowded that we could be standing right beside our blanket, looking over it, but never see it until someone would say, "Here we are." When that happened, it was always funny, and a common thing for everyone except boyfriends and girlfriends, who would be making out. Even if they went into the water separately, they never lost where their blanket was. It was one of those things that made the beach the beach. You were really not allowed to bother them or the lifeguards. The lifeguards were very high up on their tower, so it was difficult to talk to them anyway, and really, they never spoke to anyone but other lifeguards.

The sections of the beach were named with letters or numbers, which identified sections where huge pieces of wood named groynes (we called them pilings) extended from the sand past any incoming tide, and ended out in the deep water. They held the beach together so it didn't wash all the sand out when there was storms or turbulence. The pilings were another signpost, but we knew never to swim too close to them, because that was where rip tides could grab you. And you never wanted to get slammed into one by a wave.

If you saw your section by the signposts, it was safe to get through the crowds without becoming separated or lost. That was where my thoughts would go while walking the road to get there. These prime spots could be found only if you searched fast. Whoever saw one first would point it out or run to it first and drop their stuff down, waiting until the rest of the gear was brought. Then the bag was opened, and the blanket shaken in the windy air. You had to be careful not to allow it blow away, and to hold it by the corner (and then put a shoe on that corner) so it didn't blow away. This had to be done for each corner, and that marked your own personal space. It was a very happy time unless someone was blasting music you didn't like nearby—then you just tuned it out, or waited for someone to move near you who played louder music that you *did* like, if you hadn't brought your own radio. Music played a part in where you put your blanket down. Once there, you knew there was a chance that it might not be as good as you thought it was, and you go into groundhog position looking for another.

While gearing up to start the search, we would stick so close together that whatever we were carrying would bang together. While this was annoying because of the weight and the heat, our own safety made it worth it, because we were together and on the lookout for a prime real estate: a patch of sand as big as your blanket. We had a common purpose. What made it so much fun was that every single person on the crowded beach shared the exact same experience.

When we had found our spot, and it wasn't an annoying place next to a difficult neighbor, everyone around us would give a smile. We'd greet one another in victory, then give each other privacy. Then we were on the beach and it was all ours—our own little piece of solitude with the sound of the ocean in our ears, which would begin to roar and crash the closer we got to it. A bed of warm sand could be molded to your exact comfort underneath you that gave way to your every desire—it even provided a pillow.

Then there was the emptiness of the blue sky, except if there were a few white clouds. Little planes flew by with long advertisements trailing behind them. That didn't happen often. Hearing or watching them made you feel like you could be up in that plane with the pilot, flying across the whole length of the ocean and beach. The hot sun beat down on you until it melted everything that was tight in you—and the ocean, the rhythm of its sound, took you over until it crashed out every sound of traffic that had beaten you down. Fresh, cool, strong breezes blew in off the ocean through your hair and freed you of your constraints. You had complete solitude with nature . . . with about a thousand other people just a few feet away. If you wanted some company, it was easy to just watch what was going on around you. If you didn't get lost, it was heaven.

Being disoriented made it impossible to get back to the safety of your blanket, though. You had to remember other people and children—what they looked like, and the color of blankets near you. It got so crowded that people simply standing up could hide your blanket because it was flat. Sometimes, adding to the confusion, there were two lifeguard towers, and you didn't know how far up or down the beach you had moved. This was how the skill of recognition and orientation was honed in Brooklyn. I always sucked at it. That was what the *stay within sight* rule was for; it was important for everyone who shared the inability to know their orientation if they were turned a quarter of the way around. This was how we learned the skill of the conversation that starts with "Where am I?" in Brooklyn.

Rita and I would put our blanket and belongings in their proper place, strip down to our bathing suits, and slather up in Coppertone suntan lotion. Once I had fixed the sand into a comfortable position and laid down, I'd often realize I was hungry. I would be covered from head to toe in sand. After I'd proceeded to eat my sandwich with the required amount of sand the beach insisted I have, and after I'd drunk my cold drink with the required amount of sand in the cup and around the sides of my mouth, I was ready to think about going into the water. When you are a baby, it is introduced to you, and as you grow and get to know it better, you make friends with it. As you get to know it even more, you can't help but fall in love with it.

The Atlantic Ocean is so much fun to play in. It knocks you on your ass, fills your pants with muddy sand, slaps you in the face with freezing cold water, pulls and shoves you any way it wants, makes you strong as you learn to play and swim in it, and it always offers up the possibility of drowning. It's love at first sight, once you get over the terror. If you respect it, you can jump its waves, and it will keep you comfortable and cool from the scorching heat. It cleanses and rejuvenates you with its salty water, soothing your ears with its sound both in and out of the water. And it leaves you large amounts of space safe from danger, where you can decorate with sand.

As you learn to swim in it and grow stronger, there are new dangers you learn to keep away from. The deeper you go in past the great big crashing waves, they become just a part of the open sun and sky. You relax into the up-and-down motion and swim sideways across it. When you're coming back in, you can jump the waves right before they crash. You have to time it just right, and ride in with the crash. You can even let it hit you in the back as you run with it and out of the clearer rush of water. This takes your last breath as you laugh at becoming one with it so comfortably. If not, you are down for the count. If you are caught off guard, the waves crash in on you.

In the ocean, there is what is known as a washing machine. That's when you get caught between the crashing wave and the undertow. You get knocked down by the waves and then pulled under, spun around until you can't tell where the surface is. You can't breathe, because you have had the breath knocked out of you. If you do manage to find the surface, you are hit by another wave and tossed under until you drown. There is no fighting it. You are caught up in the cycle of the waves. This is one of the things my mother warned Rita about—to keep an eye on me.

I don't know if Rita got absorbed in her book, fell asleep, or was face down, getting the sun on her back and just relaxing, releasing the stress of the city and all its heat and concrete. As luck would have it, I got caught in the washing machine, and I was alone. I went feet over head three, then four times, without the ability to pull myself out of it because I lacked sufficient strength. I figured, *Well, this isn't going to stop.* Instead of being scared, I said to myself, *I am going to die, this should be interesting, might as well go with it,* and I passed out. When I came to, I was in some guy's arms, and he was holding me over my sister giving her a what-for, which I thought was funny because of the look on her face. All of a sudden, his chastising turned into *blah, blah, blah* because I realized I was being held tightly and safely in these really tanned, strong arms attached to this really good-looking guy. It was like the feeling of safety in my father's arms, but this guy was a lot more handsome, with no broken nose . . . though I loved my dad's broken nose. I don't know, he just wore it well. He got it boxing in the Navy.

I looked at the guy, then at Rita, as if to say, *If this is what it is to be in a handsome guy's arms, let's do that again!!!!!!!* What made it even funnier to me was the fact that if Rita had laughed, the guy would have killed her.

He realized I was awake, and I don't remember being put down on the blanket, or if he stood me up. All I knew was that the ocean produced some really beautiful stuff. I couldn't forget the feel of his strong, suntanned arms. He saved my life so I could have other interesting experiences. I was very grateful to him.

When he left, Rita asked me, "Are you all right?"

I said, "Yeah, let me dry off, and then I'll go back in the water but stay closer to the shore."

"Okay," she said.

And I said, "Okay, good."

Then I thought to myself, *That was different, and strange. Mom would have blown a fit at Rita, and no way in hell would Mom let me back into the water.* That would have made the whole day a drag.

I had so much fun with Rita. She was just so good, and she loved me so much. We were good to go. The guy had saved my life, *and* I could go back in the water. No problem. Of course, we never told Mom about it. It was just another fun relaxing day at the beach. Now, when I remember my reaction to dying, I think: *that was interesting*. I hope when I do die, I do it with the same curiosity.

CHAPTER 6

Learning to Run Downhill

I WAS SO SECURE, and took for granted the love shown to me before I was nine. It was even all right that I didn't like everything my family did, that I felt depleted from traveling back and forth every week, and that I was disappointed and wounded by the lack of education from members of the family who did not live in Grandpa's home, but showed up anyway, like Uncle Jimmy. Corruption and violence came so close, but never really touched my immediate family who lived with Grandpa.

I wasn't even safe from it in Mill Basin. As I got older, my Uncle John, my mom's sister Aunt Cathy's husband, was jailed for forgery. His side of the family was involved with a candy union. They had a lot of candy around the place, and rarely offered any. If it was offered, you had better know it was a sacrifice and a forced thing on their part. Having candy was when you asked for money and then bought it. It always tasted better, anyway, like my Devil Dogs or Juicy Fruit gum, because it was done with a touch of love. Uncle John also taught me how to ride my first bike: a little red one. He taught me in the backyard.

There was no going to their house and giving or getting a hug. You never kissed Uncle Johnny, and Aunt Cathy would turn her cheek unless she was giving you a Christmas gift or birthday gift. This was not like the family I was used to, where hugging was always welcome (you could even give Aunt Camy a hug, and she never got cold). To me, it seemed like this aunt and uncle's love was rarely free. It was like a forgery, especially if other people were around. They were always secretive, fantasy-based, and acted so much sweeter than they actually were. You never really existed when you were with them; you weren't important. Only they were. It felt cold and untrustworthy, with no real family connection.

We had a hill in our backyard, from which you could drive a car down into any of the garages. When I was very young, there was a girl on the block I really liked. I loved playing with her, but for some reason, my cousin Janet, who was two years older than I was, did not like her. One day, when she was playing at the top of the hill, Janet bullied me to take a pin and stab her with it. She said, "I don't like her. Stab her with it." She didn't let up until I had done it, and I never played with that nice little girl again. That was the cost of having a friendship with Janet. If I brought these things up, she would say it had been my choice, my decision to do it.

At my grandfather's funeral, Janet bullied me to steal a dime from the St. Jude's fountain because she wanted to see what the Kotex box looked like from the machine in the ladies' room.

I told her, "You do it."

"No, I couldn't do that. You do it, I am too scared. I would never do that. Someone might see me, I'll get into trouble. They won't say anything if you take it."

On and on it went. She wouldn't let up until I did it.

As an adult, I still felt so guilty that I had taken something that should have gone to save a child's life from cancer that I put more dimes back in the fountain than I normally would have, had I never stolen that dime. Chances are, she would take the credit for that, too . . . as if there were any.

Once, when we were shopping at the local drugstore as teenagers and waiting for medicine for someone, I started thinking of all the things Janet had made me do that I would never have done on my own without her "friendship." I took something off one of the shelves and stuck it in her bag when she wasn't paying attention. When she opened it to pay for her item and saw the stolen item, it was pure confusion and deep surprise. In the split second when she realized I had done it, I just smiled. I know she never forgot it, and quite possibly never forgave me. If the staff had seen it, she would have been accused of stealing, and I would have laughed at her and totally denied having anything to do with it. The guy at the counter didn't notice, but when I saw her nervousness, fear, and insecurity—the thought of being labeled as a thief, something she would never do—it became a shared experience between us as "friends." That was the first and only time I ever did this, and it was one of the most fun things I did at that age. I remember the look on her face. "Laura, what did you do? I could have gotten in trouble—they would think I stole it!" Yep, it was something she would never do. I never said I wasn't a little twisted.

This kind of thing was often called for when I was around Janet and her side of the family. Once, Janet, her cousin, some other neighborhood kids, and I were playing tag with both basement garage doors open. We were all running so fast around that big circle: from the outside, through the connecting door, and then outside again. The adults were sitting under the cherry tree enjoying themselves. As I ran full speed ahead through the doorway and into the garage, Janet's cousin Theresa slammed the garage door with its big iron handle right on top of me. It split open my left eyebrow. Of course, I started screaming, and blood was pouring down my face. When my Dad, Uncle Johnny, and Al, a neighbor, heard me, they all came running over and rushed me into the kitchen on my grandmother's side of the house. As they lifted my head up, trying to see what the wound looked like through the blood they were holding back with a cloth, my dad said, "She'll probably need stitches." Uncle John and Al agreed. Then Al said, "Lets' try a butterfly bandage; it might work. I have one." Again, they all agreed. As we waited for Al to get back, the men teased me about being able to take a good shot. They made me feel like one of the guys because they were talking about shots they had taken, and weren't lying. I don't remember which of the guys put the bandage on, or if two of them had to do it in order to keep the wound closed. My eyes were closed, too, and I had to be really still. They were still telling me about the shots they had taken themselves, as if this was nothing unusual in life.

Something welled up from deep inside my gut. I felt it travel up, then it came out. It was the first time I said *fuck* out loud, or even silently. The expletive was a combination of "What the hell just had happened to me?" and feeling sorry for myself because I was going to have a deep scar on my eyebrow. This was my real first impression of Theresa, and there was no love in it. None of these guys who were cleaning me up and putting me back together said a word about my language. I think that surprised me even more than taking a hit to the head with a massive iron handle. This allowed me to grin a little that I had gotten away with that one, and they all looked at me in agreement to boot! I laughed. Years later, I still nursed resentment toward her.

I might have been in my late thirties or even forties when Aunt Cathy and Uncle John gave a party. I walked in at the front of the house, said hello to the people I knew, and headed inside to see who was there. On my way to getting a cold drink, I was hoping they had Coke on ice. Mom still never kept it in the house. In the kitchen area, I saw Janet's cousin sitting down, glued to this guy. I looked at her, stone-faced. She was the last person I ever expected to see. She must have seen me, or been expecting to see me. As I passed by, she said hi, and I returned her greeting. She looked at the nice-looking guy next to her and said, "This is my fiancé." I'm sad to say I don't remember his name. He said hello, and was open and friendly. He had a nice smile and seemed like a good person, not at all slimy, like someone I would expect her to marry. I don't even know if they ever married.

Then Theresa's fiancé looked at her, giving her a sideways push. I remember he had a glass in his hand. I was on my way to get something cold to drink myself, and still wanted it. This was a delay on my path. She attached herself physically to this guy's arm, like she couldn't stand on her own two feet if she tried, almost crawling up him. She couldn't have latched herself onto him any closer than if she had been sweat on his upper arm. Theresa cringed, looked at my eyebrow, and said, "I am sorry I did that." She was giving me a shaky smile and speaking as if embarrassed. Then shrugged and put her head down in shame, as if she had come to grips with the idea that that was what kids did. He gave her another little shove. She picked her head up and said, "I did it because I didn't like you."

I remembered being quiet that day—just stepping back and watching her to see what she was like. I had never known her or that side of the family very well, or played with anyone in her family before that day. I just said, "Hmmm," and remained stone-faced, watching Theresa and her fiancé and thinking. Then I saw that he might have convinced her to make that apology, under the unspoken threat of either seeing her character or eventually leaving her because of it. She hadn't said this in conversation between just the two of us, assuming (or probably fearing) that I would return the favor of giving her a scar without the need for an iron door handle. It looked like in her mind, she thought she deserved it, which would not have been my reaction. I would have respected her courage and liked her for it, and we would have become friends.

I knew I would have to think about what she had said. I turned to walk away from them, but before I did, I just gave him a look, with a nod toward the little weasel still latched onto his arm. My look said, "She acts nice to get what she wants; she'll never change. Maybe she will develop honest courage?" He gave a barely perceptible smile and shrug, as he didn't know, either.

"Wish you well," was the last thing I said to him, without uttering a word. Then I walked away, and let all the resentment go. A wound deeper than flesh needed to heal. Now I understood what she was like. Yes, she had apologized, because she realized how much she had hurt me, both physically and socially. I was reminded of this every time I needed to use eyebrow pencil to fill in that scar. Yes, she meant that apology; I saw it really bothered her from the minute she realized what she had done. I knew she felt guilty just as long as I had harbored that resentment. I needed to see and hear what she had experienced, and why. It restored my faith in civilization. I was very grateful I had met her fiancé. He was a conduit. God did allow me miracles when I really needed them. I was never allowed to become completely hopeless. The rest of it wasn't my business—how she behaved toward anyone else after that. If I never saw her again, I would be happy, even if she developed some legs under her and acquired her own two feet. If I never saw him again, that would be a shame, as I would want to tell him that I admired his gentleness, courage, strength, and honesty, and would always keep him in my prayers of joy. He was a gift; I will never forget it. Brooklyn was a nice place to live. Nice things happened in it.

My cousins from Uncle Benny's family were four boys plus JoJo. Love overflowed with them, and still does: smiles and hugs that last forever, laughter, music and singing with guitars, good food, and sharing openly and honestly about everything and anything.

Of course, I loved Uncle John's sister, Aunt Anita, and her husband, Uncle Gene. I loved Uncle Gene for his gentleness and sensitivity. Aunt Anita was built like Aunt Camy: tall and solid, with darker hair and a raspy voice from smoking, like so many of the era. She was a lot mellower and funnier than Aunt Camy, though, and so much more approachable. Aunt Anita loved the ironies of life, and never shied away from laughing about them, either. You could trust her with anything, and she genuinely cared. Uncle Gene was shorter than she was, and built with a smaller frame. There was no looking at that man without thinking, *what a gentle, nice guy.* Dark hair, big dark eyes, good looking, definitely Italian, but one of the physically finer ones, far from a brute. The two of them owned a racehorse. I thought they shared the heart of a race-horse: strong, gentle, fun.

Uncle Gene and Aunt Anita had five red Doberman Pinchers that made a huge amount of noise when you rang the doorbell, but as soon as you got into the house, it was a fight between them as to who got petted and kissed first. They would all lie on the sofa at once . . . kind of a Doberman pileup. They were big dogs, and took up a lot of room in the kitchen, too. When I was there, she wouldn't let them in the kitchen with us. Aunt Anita made me feel like I was the only living thing in existence and the only thing that mattered. She would look me in the eyes with her cigarette permanently between her fingers, just like my dad—always smoking one—then lean back comfortably in her chair, and ask, "How are things with you, Laura?" She expected an honest answer.

I would go visit Aunt Anita sometimes when I walked to the stable in the neighborhood near her house to give the horses carrots, apples, and sugar cubes. When I was upset, even if I didn't tell her all of what was bothering me, I think it would have fallen out anyway with so much crying. Not a word was misunderstood, and I knew she would have done anything and everything in her power to help me. Sometimes, I couldn't find the words to convey all the sorrow and confusion I was experiencing, but she always knew when I was hurting, and just being with her was a strong comfort.

Good or bad, there was genuine love, no matter how limited, with every member of my family—except Uncle Jimmy. And they told me he loved me? I remember one time when there was an experience of a heartfelt love between Janet and me, open and honest. It's true—people aren't all good or all bad. We are so much more complicated than that. Children are children, and they are not directly involved in adult goings-on. Sometimes, children tended only to be loved because they were children, especially if they were seen and not heard. Still, it kept the will to live alive.

Grandmother Josephine seemed to bridge it all. Grandfather Al and Grandma Jenny loved her and what she had created. All of my mom's family—Grandma Josephine, Grandpa Peter, Aunt Cathy, Uncle Johnny, Uncle Benny, Aunt Helen, and my cousins lived in two attached houses. My grandfather Al, my dad's dad, loved visiting Grandma Josephine and eating the dinner she had prepared for him and set out on the picnic table under the cherry tree. To Grandma Josephine, her children were her children, and she loved them no matter what. My mom was devoted to her. Grandma Josephine made all the curtains in the house, and I later found out she made our pillowcases from the sheets corpses had been wrapped in. She didn't suffer a horror, though, because "Every penny saved is a penny earned." I got over the gag effect and just decided to not think about it. The more they got washed, the more the realization faded.

After Grandpa Peter passed when I was nine, my mom didn't want my grandmother to be left alone in her apartment too much. Early every morning, as soon as it got warm enough, Grandma Josephine was one of a kind, she would go into her garden in the backyard and work on it until she had sweat beading on her face—so much so that she needed to wipe it off, usually with a colorful half-apron with little colored flowers or a bold pattern. She wore them over her full skirts, which always came to the middle of her calves: solid skirts, and, as the weather got colder, heavier ones. Never black. I don't know if she made them all, but most likely she did. It was a guarantee that she had made all her aprons.

As soon as it got warm enough, Grandma sat in one of those metal chairs that were painted various colors: sometimes brick-red Rust-Oleum, but mostly I remember green. They were iron, with high backs and armrests. They didn't have four legs like regular chairs; they had two bars under the seat that came down, curved around, and met in the back. Even though they didn't have rockers, there was stiff support under the chair so you could push your weight back in the seat. They gave enough that they would push back and kind of rock, which was fun.

The chairs had embellishments on a semi-oval back. They were wide, with slight grooves at the top and front that allowed air in so you didn't leave behind flesh from the hot iron, should the chair be left out in the sun too long. When they were hot, you had to sit on the very tippy edge and wait for them to cool off. These heavy chairs were dragged across the cement and put under the shade of the cherry tree, which grew so high that the top was full-on bird territory. We had the bottom, and we and the birds tried to outsmart each other to get the cherries in the middle of the tree first. I must have passed underneath that tree a million times, and I always thought of the beauty, the birds, and the fight for the cherries. Grandma had a swing in the tree for us kids. I love that cherry tree. Only God could make something like that: beautiful, with white flowers and petals, and useful, nourishing, and sweet on top of it all. Even today, I have a medium-sized branch cut into logs sitting in my living room as part of my home. One has a deep red center that never lets me forget the beauty of its life. It gave life just by being.

Grandma would rub olive oil on her face, arms, and legs because it tanned better than tanning lotion and kept her skin soft. There was more ozone then, and it was okay—it wasn't a dangerous thing to do. She would be a deep golden brown by the end of the summer. Once the sun got too hot, she was in for the day. After her nap and lunch, she was ready to sit in her wooden rocking chair in front of her living-room window, on the first floor looking out onto the street.

My grandmother, Josephine Scardino, was one of a kind. After 3 P.M., you could go there and usually find her arguing the same arguments she maintained with people who were long dead. At those times, Mom wanted me to go and spend time with her. In winter, she would wear heavy socks, a button-down woolen sweater, and heavier skirts. I distinctly remember a brown woolen skirt with a blue-grey cardigan. After hearing the same stories over and over again, it was easy to want to strangle her for repeating them so often. This was a shared laugh among cousins, because every one of us wanted to do the same thing except JoJo, who was named after her. JoJo would just laugh. She might have been laughing at us, too, because she loved her Grandma Josephine in a special way: she was named after her, and they had a special bond. "You never know," JoJo laughed. "We might turn out like her, too." No one ever really tired of the stories. I wanted to record them, and regret never having done so. I always thought there would be enough time.

When she was in her mid-to-late eighties, I asked her, "Grandma, would you marry, have children, and do it all over again?"

She stopped, gave it some thought, and said, "No. I would buy a car, travel across the United States, and see all of it. I would love 'em and leave 'em."

"Enough said, Grandma."

All of this happened long after something that took place downtown when I was a child that would impact my relationship with my father and family as well as the rest of my life. I can only put it this way.

There was a plaque on the Atlantic Bank a couple of blocks up that memorialized George Washington. I passed it all the time, and had no clue why there would be a plaque of Washington on a horse there. Reading it never made any sense to me, but I finally found out why. On August 27, 1776, right after the Declaration of Independence was signed, some of our guys in Brooklyn took shots at two British soldiers who were foraging for watermelons. The American Revolutionary War was on.

The British had about 40,000 men in and around Brooklyn. Washington had about 9,000. Half of all his troops were in Manhattan. Long story short: all hell broke loose. On August 28, within twenty-four hours, Washington, in his first battle command, watched the Battle of Prospect Park, the loss of the Maryland 400, and the Battle at Gowanus Swamp, where we were drowned and crushed. The casualties were up there with Gettysburg's. If you know the layout, you know that Washington was completely surrounded, with the East River at his back. In other words, we were dead in our tracks, and the Revolutionary War could have started and ended in these twenty-four hours.

But . . . General Howe called back Cornwallis's Grenadiers, plus the 33rd foot. Howe held back because he remembered how the British had been crushed at Bunker Hill, and decided his men needed to rest that night. He would attack in the early morning, with his men refreshed and ready to defeat Washington and the rest of our remaining troops. His men knew if they advanced right then and there, it would be over.

Washington, seeing that Howe wasn't advancing, muffled all the wheels on anything that moved, kept the campfires burning, ordered his men not to talk, keep the horses quiet, and sent for longboats from the Bronx to take the wounded. He called all available boats from the Bronx, Manhattan, and Jersey, and escaped to Manhattan. None of those places are far away via water. There was inclement weather that night, and a fog rolled in through the early morning. Washington escaped the fate of losing the Revolutionary War. Even though the British held Manhattan for eight years, the war was not over. From this battle, Washington got a reputation for really stinking at commanding.

And that was just how I felt at home. I was

surrounded on every side, and the security I had come to know was being crushed and humiliated beyond belief. I had very few resources, and no way out. It took decades for me to recover from the loss and shame.

Dad was having a nervous breakdown. It doesn't seem as bad today, now that mental health issues are more accepted. There are so many resources available, along with specialized medication with fewer side effects. But in the mid-1960s, a nervous breakdown was like having a handicapped child: it was hidden. Really hidden. The unspoken chorus was that affected families "should be ashamed." You became a social outcast. But there was no hiding Dad. The only mental institutions at the time were reputed to be houses of horror, and care was limited. Dad received shock treatment while fully awake.

It started out with him saying inappropriate things. He began talking incessantly; then he wanted to fight. I remember sitting at the kitchen table at Grandpa's with Dad standing in the kitchen doorway, putting on whatever good watches he had. He went out "looking to be robbed" so he could "beat someone up" for a purpose. I didn't know what was happening. I was told to leave the kitchen. "Go watch TV," Mom said.

All Dad wanted to do was fight, and he actually was arrested once for the fighting. I didn't even know he was in jail for days. We were kept at home, and thought maybe Dad was working. I don't remember how long he was in jail, but I do remember cousin Philly being over at Grandpa's house. Philly was telling the adults that he was bringing him really good food from the restaurant, and not to worry. That was when I was informed of my father's whereabouts. Apparently, he had attacked the cops. Once he was home again, he hated cops with a passion. I don't know what they did to him, and honestly, I don't want to know. I think they beat him up in return.

I couldn't do anything to help, or change anything that was happening around me. When he acted like that, anyone under thirty left the vicinity. It was happening too fast for me. I was still being shuffled back and forth, and was still expected to do well in school. Dad had verbal fights at home and verbal fights downtown, usually started by him or by someone trying to get him back to normal. No one had ever seen anything like this before. No one knew what to do. None of the kids got remotely close enough to fight with him verbally. We weren't seen or heard.

I remember Mom saying, "He's not sleeping. I can't get him to stay home long enough to sleep. He is going to hurt himself or someone else." This was usually when she was on the phone or talking to Aunt Cathy, her sister. Not to us, of course. In reality, none of the adults were sleeping, because they were trying to stop him from getting hurt or hurting someone else. The children were so upset, sleeping was just shutting off until you had to wake up and endure another day. Every one of the adults in the family was fighting to stop it, but there was no way it was stopping. A neighbor came by downtown and talked to the adults about what my dad was doing outside, asking if he could help. Eventually, Mom told me that the neighbor's brother had had a breakdown, so he knew what our family was going through.

God knows what Dad was doing and saying to the families who came for funerals. I didn't even want to think about it, I was so embarrassed. All I knew was that Joanne wasn't taking it too well. She was really upset. It changed her forever, too, and not for the better. I think Joanne was the most sensitive of the three of us. Rita just loved my father; she stood by him no matter what. She seemed to take the stance that it would work itself out, and the love she and my parents shared would never be weakened, but only grow stronger—no matter what. She wasn't wrong.

Mom finally got him to see our family doctor. She later told me, "Doctor Greenberg wanted to put him in the hospital, and just sedate him so his body could rest. He had been working so hard, for so long, and it took its toll. But Grandpa said he had to be a man and act like a man—no hospital." Man, I knew nothing of that. Talk about not knowing what to do. It was happening too fast to even comprehend. My mom didn't win on that argument; Dad never went to the hospital to simply rest. At the time, you weren't a man if you had a nervous breakdown. Work would solve it.

I was kept out of everything, and only learned the details years later. I do remember that my father wouldn't take pills to make him sleep. I could guess that they didn't do a very good job of it anyway, as they would just slow him down—then he'd leave the house, talking a mile a minute. I remember my mom saying "Leo, please, take the pills. They will help you to relax." He was drinking coffee like mad, too. Then Mom got the idea of crushing up the pills and putting them in his coffee. This way, she could get him to take them without him knowing it. The hammer and wax paper were always out, except when my father was in. Little packets were hidden and kept where the coffee cups were. Mom was terrified that he would see her opening them over his coffee cup. He often wondered why the coffee was so bitter.

Once, a married couple came over and had dinner with us in Mill Basin. I remember watching the wife. She would be talking, and then fall asleep as she was talking. She would be listening, then her head would bob, and she would be sound asleep. She had narcolepsy. The world was becoming like some kind of bizarre circus.

The next day, I was out of the way listening to one of my mother's phone calls. She said, "Rosa called today, and said they almost got into an accident going home last night. Vincent kept falling asleep at the wheel, and they didn't know why. I must have given him Leo's pills by mistake." I stood there imagining what that would look like: he would fall asleep, she would fall asleep. How would she know he was sleeping, if she was sleeping, too? Both bobbing their heads... was it like taking turns? I gave up after a while.

I told no one at school what was happening in my home life—even Annie, who was really the only friend I had, and who came over after school sometimes. No one knew. I knew the adult neighbors knew, because they asked what was happening. I hid anytime I could once that started. I couldn't stand the stares, and would just slip off into the house or drag my mother to leave. I don't think I even cried outwardly. I went into some kind of shock. I just shut up and watched and listened to whatever I could that didn't make it worse.

Then there was a whole ruckus, with happy, sad, relieved, and worried feelings flying everywhere. Dad was going into a mental institution, and no one knew for how long. I'll never forget North Shore Mental Hospital on Long Island. Isn't it funny that I ended up going on my honeymoon nearby? It was a beautiful place across the water from the Hamptons, but with less money . . . just beaches, locally-caught fresh fish and lobster, and antique stores. The area had a sailing history. It was so quiet, and Rob's dad loved it there. I had never been, and I don't regret spending my honeymoon there at all. It was a big healing for me.

Once Dad had gone into the mental institution, everything slowly calmed down and fell into a silent routine. No more fighting at all, just some yelling left over about not understanding why he had done that, or about what should have been done. The adults were happy that they had found a good place, and that he hadn't been put into one of those nightmare places.

We didn't go downtown so much after that. Everyone needed their own space to decompress. I never made the eighty-five average that had been demanded of me every semester by my dad, and of course still was. And there was no reason I shouldn't have. "It is your only job! That is all you have to do!" he would say. He wasn't dead yet, and neither was Aunt Camy. Some semesters, I wasn't even close, as a matter of fact. I never attained that average until I went to St. John's University at age forty. Nobody could figure out why I couldn't do it. "You're smart enough to," they'd say. That was when depression first started to settle into me and take hold in such a way that it even eventually changed the construct of my brain. Like a physical brain injury.

One thing struck me so hard, it was like the worst physical blow I had ever taken. It was a holiday, and my dad had come home. We had dinner at Grandpa's house in the living room again, with the table with all the leaves put in it. Dad had invited a younger guy he had made friends with at the hospital over for dinner. Dad kept saying, "He is a nut like me. Anthony is a nut like me." We used to joke and call each other nuts and laugh. This time, no one was laughing. He was so dead serious. It just crushed me. Dad's sense of humor had changed forever. He would never again be the father I once knew. His experience had changed his whole demeanor. Anthony was a nice guy: good looking, quiet, nice smile. Dad had brought him home to meet Rita. I laughed about that, but I think it was the only time I did. It was not a happy laugh, either. She did go out with Anthony a few times, and said, "He was a nice guy."

My sisters and I never talked about what was happening to my dad. It was still *children are seen and not heard* time. That seemed to last forever. I also think it was way too painful for us. No one knew how to approach it. Counseling for children, as far as I knew, was unheard of at the time, and Mom certainly didn't have the time or the ability to hold it all together and to take me and/or Joanne, too. It was assumed that you knew how to handle it on your own. And when it was over, it was in the past—no need to bring it up.

I know Dad's mental illness changed his relationship

with his sister, Aunt Camy. And that changed my mom's relationship with Aunt Camy, Grandma, and Marie. She, like me, missed Marie terribly. I knew they loved each other still, but no one was the same. Dad had bad back injuries from falling off a ladder, but this had injured the whole spine of the family. A fracture had occurred. I know there was blame, and things were said in anger—different perspectives that no one had enough tolerance to give thought to, things that were just not understood.

Many years later, when I was working with Dad, someone—I believe it was Butch, a friend of my dad who was also a funeral director, and owned the livery company the hearse and limousines were always rented from—showed me a picture of my father at his office desk. He had black-rimmed glasses on, and it looked like he was studying something. I didn't recognize him. It had been taken without his knowledge, and he looked so calm and kind of philosophical, like a teacher or professor studying something with deep interest and intelligence. I don't think anything like his breakdown would have happened if my dad hadn't had to do so much, with no one to help him share the emotional burden. I knew the picture had been taken after his breakdown. Because I was kept so far out of his life by this time, I didn't want any part of it; it scared me so much. I couldn't even hug my dad anymore. I didn't know him. This photo was the only thing I could hold onto that had no pain in it—something I could look at and study by myself, to get to know my dad as his friends knew him, to see why they loved him. That was the only memory I have of that entire time that does not hurt, and it only lasted a few minutes.

Somehow, things got cobbled together again. Dad went back to work on a consistent basis. We were going back and forth downtown on a regular schedule again.

My cousin Marie, who was devastated by all of it— her face just showed it—met Steve, and they became engaged. Steve was not from New York, and he was tall and thin with blonde hair and blue eyes. He didn't have an accent, but looked Midwestern. He was in the Coast Guard.

Marie never talked to me about what had happened in the family, but she always managed to take me away from these painful experiences through things I would never forget, the kind that would change my life for the better. That doesn't mean things got better, though. She just allowed me a breather.

CHAPTER 7

Marie's Wedding

WHEN MARIE GOT ENGAGED, things started to change. There was more activity in the house, and it wasn't devastating.

One day, Marie said to me, "Would you like to go out with me and Steve?"

Rita took me out with her boyfriends all the time, or let me hang out with them, and sometimes got ticked or annoyed at having me around. When I got overtired and was being bratty, even I didn't want to hang out with myself, so I knew how they felt. But Marie? That was unheard of. She never once got annoyed or angry with me. So of course, I jumped at the chance with surprise, and a feeling of pride being out with her and a guy in a sailor's uniform. There was a specialness and a twinge of timidity within me . . . but being timid only lasted about twenty seconds.

I had no clue where we were going, but I was "dressed properly," according to my mother. We got into Steve's car and drove for about twenty minutes. Then Steve probably felt like strangling me, because I was sitting in the back seat of the car with my arm out the window, playing with the wind. This was not his idea of fun, considering the fact that there was traffic flying by. He kept saying, "PUT YOUR ARM BACK IN THE CAR!!! YOU COULD GET HURT!!!!"

"Okay" was my response, and within five minutes, my arm was back out the window again. It started out slowly: first my fingers, with a life of their own, would feel the wind, then the tip of my palm, and before I could help it, my whole arm was stretched out, riding the waves of the wind, which was the best thing to do in a car that was going fast.

I thought to myself with annoyance, *So what? There's traffic. There is always traffic. Nothing new!* Then again, maybe Marie would never take me out with her and Steve again.

"Put your arm back in!"

Then with exasperation, because he wouldn't stop telling me that, plus I didn't know why he was getting soooo annoyed with me, the thought came to me: *Aww, he's just not from New York. Has no clue how to live. Losing a limb is a part of the game. The worst that could happen is a serious UH OH.* Flying down the highway with my arm stretched out, I visualized it being swiped off and blood flying all over the place. It was kind of cool. He had no clue how to relax.

Marie knew me. She was from New York, and just out of trying to act like it was the right thing to do, she asked me once to put my arm back in the car. It calmed him down, he thanked her; then out went my arm again. I heard a growl under his breath. Didn't he know I was a kid, and this was like the only thing we could do to enjoy ourselves in a car when there was wind? Reading in the car made me puke—I didn't think he wanted that. He was just so annoying. He would have had no ability to be from New York, even if he wanted to. Actually, I felt bad for him. *Poor guy, what a shame*, came the thought. I wanted to tell him, "Relax! Being a kid will eventually stop in about fifty or sixty years, maybe." I loved the feeling of the wind.

He started looking right and left, busily looking for an exit, and all of a sudden we were at a parking lot. We got out of the car and quickly had to pick up the pace. We walked as fast as we could across it, and it wasn't a small thing. I didn't know where we were, and had no reference point. Then, stunned, I saw a speedboat with another sailor on it. We were going on it!!!! We were going out on the ocean!!! Wow, Marie had topped it all. We were going on a Coast Guard boat!

We got onto the boat. I was told, "Leave everything alone, don't touch anything." I stood up at attention and did nothing, just watched us pulling away from the pier in any way I could see it, giving Steve space to work the way he needed to. We started picking up speed. The other sailor was huffing and puffing. He had pulled the ropes back in, and had put his back to me. I got it—what he was doing was really important, so leaving him alone was probably the best thing to do. But he hadn't even smiled a hello to me. He was totally ignoring me, as if I had no right to be on the boat at all.

This made me feel even prouder that I was on it. It was more special than I could ever have imagined. It was sunny and beautiful that day. As soon as we were far enough from the dock, we started to move even faster. I didn't want to stay in the cabin. I wanted to sit at the front of the boat and get a full view of everything, just taking it all in. I knew I would never be able to do this kind of thing ever again. I was on a Coast Guard speedboat. I wanted to be bounced around by the water, hanging on, feeling the power of the boat and the water, the skill of Steve driving it. It was even a friend of ours driving it! He must have been happy that my arm hadn't gone flying off in the car.

Marie disappeared for me; she just let me feel that I was fully free to enjoy it any way I wanted on that boat. I would not be held back; she trusted me. So I asked if I could sit outside at the front, as close as I could get. Steve said, "Sure, but you have to be careful. Go slow." *Yea!!!!* was my thought. *I will never feel this wonderful again.* I had been allowed on a boat that wasn't just for fun. It had a purpose; and not only that, it could come up and face something really dangerous. These guys were in uniform. It was the first time I felt so proud to be an American. There was no danger. It was safe, and it was fun. I completely forgot about home. I was breathing in some powerful, fresh air.

Steve told the other sailor, "Go with her," but the guy wanted no part of me. I hadn't done anything that I knew of to get him so disgusted and mad so soon. He didn't know me that well yet.

He made sure I was safe, and that I wouldn't be bounced off the boat. Then he just stared straight ahead. I'd had it with this guy. I thought, *If he wants to be so mad, let him enjoy it.* As long as he was keeping me safe, he could be as miserable as he wanted, I didn't care. I was going to full-out enjoy myself and this ride.

Then I got bored with him being so quiet, so I asked him a benign question to feel him out. He answered my question. Then I made a statement about how beautiful everything was. He WAS a nice guy, but not so overly handsome that he was more handsome than his uniform. I wasn't intimidated, and I was going to talk to this guy whether he liked it or not. There was no way in hell I could stay that silent while being with someone. People were just too interesting. It was getting dull being with him, so after a few more questions and statements from me, he started breathing more comfortably, like hot steam had been released.

When I knew he would talk to me, I asked him, "Why don't you like me?" He took a breath in, thought about it, decided to talk, and said, "Steve told me he was bringing a really beautiful girl with long brown hair today, and that she had these really beautiful brown eyes, and chances are she would really be interested in me. He said he knew you, and there would be no doubt." I took the compliment with gratitude. I had never been described that way before, that I knew of. When I realized what he had said, I nearly fell off the boat laughing to myself. I would NEVER have laughed at him. It was a mean thing for Steve to have done. I was ten.

I said, "I'm sorry he did that to you; it wasn't fair." I really meant it, too.

After that, we were friends. He answered any questions I had, willingly kept me safe, and acted warmer, not so angry. He liked me better. He seemed to want to just shrug—he knew we wouldn't be on the boat the whole day. It seemed like he was already on the boat a lot, and it didn't hold THAT much interest.

I put my face back into the wind, felt the sun on my shoulders, and looked back at him with really big smiles, acknowledging that he was so lucky and really special for protecting the country like he was doing— even the tension of putting his life on the line. I was very sensitive to the sense of actual death. It was a huge thing, and I wasn't the only one who was grateful. The entire country was, and that felt like the whole world. I was privileged to be with him and on that boat even just for that one day, and he knew it.

I could take my attention off the wind and skyline, and pay attention to how the boat was being maneuvered under my feet, too. It had a power and a life of its own that responded willingly to do its job with everything it had. It was wonderful. I can still see the blue sky, and feel the sun on my shoulders and the wind on my face.

When we got home that day, it had drained me of everything that hurt—and it still does, for as long as I think about it again. When some time had passed, I told my dad what Steve had done. Dad said, "I don't like him. He's a smartass."

Even so, it was decided that Guy Charles, who lived in one of the apartments above the funeral home, was going to make the wedding dress. He was one of the gay guys my dad loved to rent to. Dad always said, "Gay guys keep their apartments so much better than women. The chances of neglect or spite in the apartment are nil. If I could rent them to all gay guys, it would be okay."

What was really special about Guy Charles, who was a good friend of the family, was that he had been a Trappist monk. It was the first time I had been so close to anyone who had been a monk—one of the coolest ways to be a priest of all the kinds you could be. They were self-sufficient, and sold jams and jellies all over. I could see these guys running around in their monk's robes, hoods, and long sleeves they could hide their hands in, making strawberry jam. They were probably actually in jeans and work shirts.

They were a Catholic community of cloistered, contemplative men. That meant they stayed at their monastery and prayed for you, whether they knew you or not. They had no physical dealings with people outside the monastery. Obviously, crossing the borders of society past prayer, to be self-sufficient for self-sufficiency's sake, was something extraordinary for me. I felt that their jelly was holy. Their products held a kind of reverence. I would say a silent prayer before I opened a jar of my favorite kind of jelly that I knew I was privileged to have, then smear some on my bagel with cream cheese. Mmmm. Heaven.

What I liked most about Guy Charles was that he had two first names. How cool was that? He was always impeccably dressed. He had serious class, was seriously intelligent, and had artistic talent that was a true gift. His apartment was so cutting-edge. He had a phone in the bathroom, and a round bed. He had the same lover for as long as I could remember.

Grandpa started not feeling well; they didn't know what was wrong. I think it was close to a real knock-down struggle to get him to the doctor. So, while the wedding was being planned, Grandpa not feeling well in addition to the sorrow and drain from Dad's breakdown was concerning. It seemed like the air had been punched out of my family. I guess you could say everyone was going through the motions, but the real heart of it all was gone. Although we were still going downtown, especially for the holidays, we started going less and less as time went on. Mom was starting to put unopened gifts under the Christmas tree we had at home. We usually put it up and decorated it the week before Christmas, then left and came home after New Year's Day.

After Grandpa's funeral, there was the dinner Italians share after the funeral of a loved one. The dinner is meant for remembering good times with the person, to see and have dinner with family members you hadn't seen since the last wedding or funeral, and take a breath from such a sad day without having to go home hungry and weak. Not only was it a tradition, it was an insult if it was not done, both for the family and for the deceased. If you didn't eat a good dinner together, you didn't get the physical and emotional nourishment you so desperately needed. It was completely disrespectful to the love and good memories that person's life had blessed you with.

I was at Uncle Jimmy's wake, kept it running smoothly, and was totally available if anyone needed anything. When it came to the funeral itself, and the mercy meal, I didn't go. I made sure I stayed in the funeral home and available for business. Smart, right? It was a few days after Christmas, so it was kind of guaranteed there would be three funerals that week.

Anyway, the dinner was the last time that person would be celebrated by family and friends together. After my grandfather's funeral, at the "mercy meal," I was sitting diagonally across from Guy. There was a female family member in attendance I didn't even know. When she got one look at Guy, she sat drooling in her plate throughout the whole dinner. She did everything she could to get his attention. She didn't know he was gay. We were laughing our sides out, and of course, he wouldn't be rude and laugh, too, when she said "Guy!" for the hundredth time with a raised finger. It was like she wanted to be called on in class. She sat about four people down from him, and he was so gracious to her. I could understand it, though. He was that attractive.

Of course, everyone, including Guy, was tall to me. I was only four feet tall until the fifth grade. As the years passed, his hair took on a silver shimmer. I don't remember now what his natural color was. Probably some shade of brown; I don't remember it being black. The way it greyed was captivating. Bottom line: *he* was captivating. Always trim and poised. I can't describe his features except to say that they were so well-proportioned. I always saw him as a picture—completely whole. Maybe this came from my first thought of him in monk's robes. You had to study him diligently to see all his attributes. His clothing and talent always floored me. Guy said the monks had to keep a vow of silence while they ate, and there was a big sign on the wall that said something like *Keep your damn mouth shut!* We both laughed, because he wasn't making that up.

Guy volunteered to make Marie's wedding dress. Everyone agreed it would be personally tailored only for her: a completely original handmade dress, especially the veil. The chances were 99.99% that it would be stunning. I remember Marie made it a point that she did not want pearls on it. "They bring pain and bad luck." She would not have any on her dress, or even on her veil. So of course, when I got married and designed my own wedding dress, I was going to disprove that theory. Test it to its fullest, and face it down because I didn't believe it. I made a point of it. I even had pearls throughout my veil. It was beautiful. Considering the fact that a box of spaghetti would have lasted longer than my marriage, being more curious about Marie's theory and minimizing the pearls might have been better idea.

Once I got a little older, I started being shipped off to my cousins in Long Island during the summer. This was a blessing. JoJo and I would spend hours just walking to the main road and shopping center, passing by her old high school and little stores with such wonderful things to buy. She was six years older than I was, and just a loving soul. Taller, like Rita; lighter brown hair, brown eyes, calm, thoughtful. A loving sense of humor. Gentle. She was (and still is) much like the water near where she was born—calming to me.

All of her brothers loved her. Each one of my male cousins was different from the next. The only thing they had in common was the desire to show their love and never cause trouble. They were always open, ready to talk honestly about what they thought and felt. They kept me human. Peter had the love of devotion. Ronnie was outgoing and self-reliant, never anything but straight-up honesty. Tommy was smart and a natural lover, with a smile that could melt ice, kind and gentle but also really caring. Michael was younger than me, and had deep, dark hair and deep, dark eyes like pools of the water of mercy. He didn't have a mean bone in his body (he grew to six foot two), and his eyes never changed.

My cousins always kept me grounded, happy, and safe from the outright brutality of Brooklyn. We survived it all together, and still find joy in each other's company. I watched the moon landing with them. Really special times, always. There was a canal within walking distance from their home, and Uncle Benny took us fishing all the time. You had to climb a white fence to get down into the boat. It would take me forever, because I was so scared I'd fall into the boat or the canal. It was a good-sized drop. Uncle Benny used to say, "You're like molasses in winter! Come on! Let's GO!!!" My cousins always laughed at Uncle Benny and at me as they helped me over. That always made me laugh, too, but that didn't speed me up any. Unfortunately for Uncle Benny, my cousins couldn't have cared less how long it took me, which just made it funnier. I was like one of those lizards that moves forward and backward for half an hour and gets nowhere fast.

Uncle Benny would say to me, "You always tell Aunt Helen how much you love her. What about me? I'm your uncle. Don't you love me?" As if he should be more special just because he was my mother's brother. I would say, "But Uncle Benny, I do love you. I love you for marrying Aunt Helen."

Uncle Benny was very tightly wound. It seemed as if he might explode at any minute. As a kid, he had always gotten the short end of the stick, and had a really angry relationship with his mother. He was the youngest, and she left him with my great-grandparents until she could bring him to Brooklyn. This happened when he was old enough to be more independent and participate in the household. My mother said, "He has a resentment with Grandma," but she would never tell me why—just that he had lived in Manhattan as a child. After Uncle Benny died, I was told that my great-grandparents also went out to work, and he was left on his own anyway.

I once met a woman at a retreat who told me about being used as a numbers runner when she was a little girl, on Union Street downtown. The Union Street area was where people died from lead poisoning more often than any other cause, unless they were really old women.

Uncle Benny was raised on Mott Street—the same Mott Street where the Black Hand a.k.a. Cosa Nostra a.k.a. the Mafia never left or changed. He was left there by my grandma because she had to work. As a little boy, the neighborhood didn't make him a numbers runner—they made him a gun runner. He was never suspected because he was a child.

When Uncle Benny was growing up, he found out he had a gift for massage that could unknot any tension you had in your shoulders, back, legs, etc. It never hurt, either—it always felt good when he would do that for me. It was as if he had gone to school for it. He would explain that you didn't work on the tight muscle itself, but in a different area, because that was the source of the real tension that had caused the muscle to tighten. I used to wonder how he learned, and figured he just had a natural talent and kept practicing on people he met along the way. Apparently, that's exactly what he did. He got the chance to use and hone his natural gift by massaging the stress and knots out of the prostitutes in the neighborhood when they needed it. My cousin told me Uncle Benny said, "You know, after they had a hard time of it, I could work out any pain they had, the tight muscles." Yup—what a way to develop a skill. Only God knows what else he was used for as a kid that made him such a nervous wreck. As a child, I used to assume he was so wound up because he had four boys instead of five girls.

Uncle Benny also played the guitar and the harmonica. He sang, and always kept little birds as pets. Unfortunately for him, when I stayed over, JoJo and I would keep him up until all hours of the night whispering to each other and laughing out loud. Uncle Benny would yell from his bedroom, "Will you two shut up in there!?" We would be quiet for five minutes, and then it would start all over again. I could never figure out why the guys got into trouble when we were the ones who caused it. When I was there, Uncle Benny didn't sleep all summer.

Our best memory as a group was when Uncle Benny took us to Montauk Point at the tip of Long Island, someplace by the shore, yet close to the woods. We went clamming, and had roasted corn, clams, and the rest of the food Aunt Helen and Uncle Benny brought and cooked over an open fire. The fire was made from the wood everyone had to collect. All of us remember that as the best day we ever spent together. JoJo and I found little blue flowers by a highway we came across while exploring. None of my cousins ever found that special place again, no matter how hard they tried.

Those summers saved my sanity. Then I would come back, and slowly but surely, the heaviness would come back again. New grade, new "never using her full potential," as my teachers said to my parents every parent-teacher night. "I am so disappointed in you. You are smarter than Rita! Why don't you get better grades?" my father would say every time they returned home. One year, he looked at my report card, gave me a disgusted glance, threw it on the floor, and didn't talk to me for about a month. It killed me. He just acted as if I didn't exist . . . as if his only children were Rita and Joanne. His getting meaner didn't make me do any better in school. He wasn't happy, but it wasn't just me, either. After his breakdown, he got that way with every one of the adults, too—except my mom.

He loved her until the end. I'm not so sure he didn't have sex with other women, though. When I asked my mom if he had, she said, "Italian men think they aren't men unless they have other women."

"Why don't you leave him?" I asked. "How can you stay with him?"

"It is like a callous, you just develop one."

That was another reason I never married an Italian man—not that it makes any difference. It was just something men generally thought they have the right to do. They thought they hurt no one, that it was expected of them. They were going to do it because they were men. In other words, bullshit.

It was easier just to avoid my father as much as possible, but deep down inside, I felt he had betrayed my sisters and me more than he ever betrayed our mother. I never developed a callous, will never develop a callous, and will never give one, either. Maybe I rubbed a few people the wrong way, but I thought it was better to stand independently on my own two feet without a man at my side. This required being so much stronger than any man living under the delusion of what made him a man. It required self-respect as well as respect for the dignity of others. I could never see how being married and having an affair made you feel like more of a man, especially if you had young children. Break the contract first. Have the guts to make up your mind and live by it. This was my line of thinking ever since I learned that simple lesson about betrayal. It bothers no one to have a spine, and it's certainly not because I am Catholic that I thought or felt this way. If anyone believed that, I'd have to say, "Check your delusions of grandeur." To me, it was a coward's way out of a contract. It was abusive, and more than just having a callous.

Have I ever had sex with married men? Sure, I have. I wasn't married, they were liars, and I never said I wasn't a little twisted—but not that twisted, or perfect by any means. I learned the lesson better when I behaved like a little bit of a hypocrite myself. Like I said, I wasn't married, but I had no great qualms until I realized I was taking part in things I'd sworn I'd never do. If I wanted to be able to look at myself in the mirror, it was a hell of a lot easier for me to avoid becoming an active alcoholic, or so self-centered that I didn't care how another woman was betrayed as long as I got what I wanted. At least, that's what I found. I learned a hard lesson, the mean way.

Back then, there was family tension even without my dad's help. Marie's stunning wedding dress was almost finished, the invitations sent, etc.—and Marie never married Steve. Holy cow, she was really miserable after that. I don't know why they broke up. It was considered none of my business, and I was glad; that was nothing I wanted to add to my bankbook of sorrow. I did go to her wedding reception in my twenties, though, over ten years later. She married Tom, the sweetest guy you'd ever want to meet. Just like Marie. She looked beautiful, and she was genuinely happy. I drew such a sigh of relief, and still do anytime I think of it.

And Guy Charles? The last time I heard about him was years later, when my father told me he was "an alcoholic on the Bowery." It dropped me to my knees.

And the funerals went on uninterrupted.

CHAPTER 8

A Wedding, Two Graduations, and a Funeral

WHILE MARIE WAS HEALING from making the right choice, she continued to work on Wall Street, like Aunt Camy. Marie liked her job; it wasn't a bad thing. We stayed home more often as time folded forward.

Rita dated a lot. She was beautiful. Five foot eight inches tall, and dark brown hair that could get kinky, depending on the weather. She would straighten it, and do all kinds of stuff to fit the style of the day. Everyone did. Ironing your hair was a bit touchy, but that never stopped anyone. Straight was in. If you weren't married by twenty-one, then "old maid" was a label that stuck. Some girls got away with it until they were twenty-three, but not many. Being Catholic and a virgin was usually safer, but not because it was a religious thing. I don't believe a lot of people understood the reason behind it for religious purposes: it was simpler, and you didn't have to deal with Italian fathers and their protective services. Or loss of face if it got out that you were easy, and no one would marry you.

I was told that Grandma, my father's mother, had gone completely grey by the time she was twenty-eight. She never dyed her hair. It was a pretty silver color. Back then, I wanted grey hair soon, because it was so becoming. Boy, do I regret ever wishing for that. Grandma was born in America, not Italy. She was pretty, tall and stately; a good-looking woman, but she didn't have it easy. I think her dad died—I'm not sure. I do know her mom married a bootlegger after that. I think grey hair kind of says it all; people who've gone grey never talk a lot of specifics. Grandma always told me, "You can't thread a needle if it keeps moving." I had no idea what the hell she was talking about, and asking my mother what she meant didn't help any, either—until one day, I thought, *OH*.

Rita was going with the current trend, and doing what was expected of her as a good girl: making sure her boyfriend was the right guy, the one she was going to spend the rest of her life with. She was serious; she meant it. Times were changing, but Rita wasn't.

I remember one guy Rita dated—Louie. I loved him the best of all the guys she ever dated. One night, Joanne and I were playing Mouse Trap on the kitchen table in Mill Basin. It was the best game we had. We played it all the time, especially if we wanted to have real fun. The three of us, or just two—either way. It was always guaranteed fun, no matter how many played. Dad and Rita (who was waiting for Louie to come and pick her up for their date) were watching the ball game in the living room. Dad still had to eyeball the guys Rita dated to make sure her chances of remaining safe were understood. Mom was doing her mom stuff all around the house . . . always doing something.

I heard Dad call to Mom, "Laura? Get me something cold to drink."

"Iced tea, Leo?" asked Mom.

"Okay," he responded.

Mom made the best iced tea. She made fresh black Tetley or Red Rose tea with fresh-squeezed lemon, then added some lemon slices. She never put sugar in it. If you wanted sugar, you added it to your own taste. The thing that made it so good was the amount of freshly-washed mint just picked from the backyard garden. Usually, in the early mornings, Mom would ask her mother to pick some from the garden. Grandma would come in with the mint and a few other little gifts. The surprises were whatever had ripened that morning: a few figs, or some cherries, tomatoes, or squash. She would put them in her apron, which was used as a catch-all. Grandma would pick them while she was working in the garden at about eight o'clock in the morning—still early, so they could be chilled or made to go with dinner that day.

To the tea, Mom would add some branches of mint or a bunch of leaves that had been picked off the branches. If you clipped off the top of the plant and used it, the plant would become two branches.

Grandma could prune those plants and make them grow so they lasted the whole summer . . . all you could ever want. When you took the pitcher out of the refrigerator and stirred it to make sure all the flavors were blended, then looked into the pitcher, it was a swirl of tawny liquid, kissed with yellow slices of lemon going up and down through the delicious-looking, colorful tea. The most desirable and refreshing part of it were the rough, sun-brightened green mint leaves. When you licked them, they licked you back. If the mint was in branches, it swirled at an angle. If it was in leaves, they ran around the pitcher. If you wanted any of them, you would have to chase and catch them with the stealth of a cheetah.

It was a skill to swirl and pour the tea without using a spoon to take the leaves out. That was like cheating. It was fair play if you took a slice of lemon with the spoon. As the tea was poured in your glass, fresh mint would wash over your senses first. Then the cold, which could almost be felt from afar as the glass frosted and sweated. Usually, just looking at that tawny color in the glass was as far as I got. At that point, I wasn't going to wait any longer to drink it. Even without sugar, the tea was so cold and refreshing, with all the raw flavors bursting cold in your mouth. But those leaves were tricky little buggers. You had to catch them before one escaped down your throat and choked you to death: chewing them, swallowing them, and licking your lips would prevent you from dying while drinking a glass of iced tea. Grandma always made sure we tasted life raw, in its full flavor and full danger.

Well, the knock on the door came. The dog barked, and the cat ran for its life. Everyone was in the kitchen by now, and Louie was standing in the doorway. He had curly hair that was almost black; the Italian kind of curly. It was longer than it looked, and it was beautiful. He had a thin face, a thin body, and a black goatee. Rita was thin, too, and he was about as tall as she was. For a guy in my family, five feet ten inches was short, but Louie had so much good, lively energy that he beamed. He had a natural smile, big and bright, like I'd never seen before. The goatee just cracked me up. It was the first time I had ever seen one for real. I saw my dad roll his eyes at Rita, with a silent *I can always count on you, Rita, to bring the weirdest guys home.* We all said hello. Mom offered Louie something to eat or drink—that just went with the territory. Then he noticed what was happening on the table: the Mouse Trap game. "Oh wow, Mouse Trap!" he exclaimed.

Joanne and I asked, "Want to play?"

"YEAH!" said Louie, who had been expecting to take Rita out. All of a sudden, he peeled off his jacket and sat down. We start setting up a new game.

Rita just said with a big smile, "Well, if you're going to play Mouse Trap, then I'm going to watch the rest of the baseball game." She had probably been wishing she could watch it to the end, anyway. She loved baseball. In her adulthood, even married with two children, she still had a full-sized poster of a baseball player stuck to her laundry room wall like a sixteen-year-old.

Louie said, "Sure, go ahead," with this big, excited smile as he chose the color of mouse he wanted. We had so much fun; plastic mice were being catapulted across the kitchen. We laughed so much that night. I was looking forward to him staying longer, but to my surprise, when the game ended, he and Rita left!

I never saw Louie again, and never had more fun with one of Rita's dates again, either. What a comfortable guy to be with. He could have been a brother or a friend. I think it may have been the goatee Dad didn't go for. "Beatnik." Not marriage material. But I loved the guy, and would have married him in a minute. I think my father would have had no say in the matter. That was where Rita and I differed. I was more like my dad, but being eleven years old kind of cramped my style.

Rita also dated a Southern boy, Southern drawl and all. He was great, too. He taught me how to make a whistle out of straw, and sent me birthday cards for years. Rita loved when I got along with people, even her boyfriends. Of course, I was never a threat. Joanne didn't quite feel the same way. If I became friends with one of her boyfriends, she did view it as a threat. Joanne's boyfriends were all right—nice guys—but her friend Bobby, who became like a family member, was the only one it was okay for me to be friends with. That was because she didn't want to marry him. I never liked her boyfriends like Rita's. Rita and I had more of the same taste in guys than Joanne and I did. She never trusted me—with absolutely no cause.

Once, Rita dated David, who was in the Navy band. He was big and heavy-set, with platinum blonde hair and blue eyes. He played the tuba and the piano like I'd never heard before. Rita said David could play any instrument that was put into his hands—he had such a gift. Rita wanted to learn to play the piano, and my mother had wanted to learn it her whole life, too, so Mom was on board for sure. David took Rita around to see which one had the best sound available for the money she could afford. She always made good money because of her secretarial skills and poise. Her height and beauty didn't hurt any, either. So she bought one. An upright, nothing grand, more functional; but it had a beautiful sound, and a life of its own. It was an instrument with its own voice. When it had been delivered and tuned, David sat down and played it. He played classic Chopin, then "Kitten on the Keys." Wow. Watching someone who knows how to play the piano can be an inspiration for the rest of your life.

One day, we were at home downtown, and it was just Rita and me in the house. I think everyone had gone to a wedding, and I was left for Rita to babysit. My father knew she would have David over when he had explicitly told her not to. She said to me, "Laura, David's coming over. Don't mention he was ever here."

Sounded like a plan to me. "Sure," I said. For me, keeping a secret from Dad for Rita was a high point in a dull life. David showed up with his tuba and came upstairs. He hadn't been there long before Dad came home unexpectedly because he had gotten called to work. David, who was about six foot four and close to 300 pounds, started to run around with the tuba in his hands, trying to hide in open space. Finally, Rita shoved him and the tuba into Grandpa's closet. Don't ask me how he fit. The closet wasn't that big, and Aunt Camy kept her foxes, the ones biting their own tails, in there. I knew that was an omen.

Dad came up. Rita gave me a look that said *oops, this is not going as planned.* We were both scared she would get in trouble, but dying laughing because my dad had no idea what was going on as he changed his clothes. I was picturing David in the closet: more of a sardine with a tuba. When Dad said "All right, I'm going," Rita and I looked at each other and thought, *that was close.* When my father decided it might rain, he turned around and went to get his raincoat from Grandpa's closet. Rita knew she was dead. We both knew it. Dad opened the closet door, and there was David, holding his tuba. Dad didn't say a word, neither did David—except "Excuse me" as he and his tuba squeezed past my dad. The last I saw of David was him leaving the house, walking through the downstairs door next to the funeral-home door, holding his tuba.

Dad said to Rita, "You are lucky I have to leave for work," and left. All Rita and I said to each other was, "He almost left, never knowing David was in the closet."

"I didn't expect Dad to go to the closet at all."

"Almost got away with it." Rita was lucky. All I remember was my mom doubling over with laughter when Dad told her to punish Rita. My mother could never keep a straight face even at the mention of it, and Dad would just shake his head in disbelief.

By the time things cooled off—in about ten minutes, for Rita—it became something she had gotten away with. It was just like her, getting caught with a six-foot-four guy holding a tuba in a closet that was only two by four feet. I think my dad froze faster in front of that closet than anyone he had ever put on ice.

Then Rita met Jack. Things got serious. It wasn't as if she wasn't still fun—she always was—but talking about a wedding was something different. Jack was really smart, had a gift for word play, and was just a gentle, nice guy. Tall . . . very tall. The kind of guy that the older he got, the more handsome he became. Even now, age is just showing who he really is inside: a gift of a guy.

Around the time, NASA had computers, but computers might also have been possible to buy. . . if you had a million dollars. We still had rotary phones—no cell phones. NASA owned the only computers. Not even answering machines existed, and no texting or email could be conceived of at that time. Only letter-writing, and copies made on typewriters with carbon paper between two sheets of paper. Make a mistake, and everything had to be started all over again. Nothing was open on Sundays. Everything moved a lot more slowly and nothing was 24-7. It was a nice time. People were more physically social. They played more together, socialized more together, and participated in each other's lives. The music was more acoustic, not electric-acoustic, but the sixties were happening. By the time I was in the eighth grade, nuns were no longer required to wear full habits. They shortened their veils, showed their hair, shortened their dresses, and began to leave their profession. Fewer were taking vows. More priests were leaving to get married, and not as many men were becoming priests in the first place. Things were starting to get shaky, and it was getting shaky in the family, too. The sicker Grandpa became, the more our tension neared the breaking point.

Joanne went to Woodstock when she had told my father she wasn't going to go. He wasn't having it, but she went anyway. Dad found out . . . but Joanne was not Rita. All hell broke loose. Plus, she was dating a guy my dad didn't even like.

Joanne was beautiful. She was the prom queen, got good grades at St. Joseph's High School, and was loved by both teachers and students. She had a friend from school who lived across the street. Her name was Johanna. She was Lebanese, and had had polio. One leg was a lot thinner, and she limped. What a regular sweetheart: soft-spoken, funny, thoughtful, and kind. She really liked me, and treated me like a little sister. She treated me better than Joanne.

Joanne and I had a love-hate relationship. There were times we got along great, and times we were like fire with oil thrown on it. It was like an explosion. She said she felt that being the middle child just cast her out from the family. I think Rita and I getting on so well didn't make it any easier for her. She was a serious loner, anyway. As far as Joanne was concerned, if I had never been born, life would have been a lot easier for her. Let's put it this way: she expressed that sentiment quite clearly at times, and had no problem beating me up. Once, when we were in grammar school, she had me on the floor in a corner, and kicked me in the stomach. Definitely a love-hate relationship.

It became easier when she began high school. Because it was within walking distance of my grandparents' house and Aunt Camy had loved Joanne like crazy since she was born, it was decided she would live with my grandparents during that time. Which was fine with me. It was safer.

They found out what was wrong with Grandpa. He had leukemia. If Rita and Jack were going to be married, it would have to happen before Grandpa died. He was not going to miss seeing at least one of his grandchildren be married. Things were just tense all around. Highs and lows were happening all at the same time. Joanne and I were close to graduating: Joanne from high school, and me from grammar school. Something was wrong—more wrong than I could put my finger on.

I was still sketching. Grandma Josephine taught me how to embroider by having me make a sketch on a piece of material. Then she showed me how to embroider different stitches on it. I embroidered Rita and Jack a tablecloth and napkin set. Certain things kept me content, and they didn't include school work. The entire family was making a hook rug of a sailing ship for Rita and Jack, for their wall. It took forever, but it was beautiful. American Traditional was all the rage at the time.

Somewhere deep down, I felt I was losing my moorings and being left behind. I understood that Dad felt like he was losing control of his life, too: he started to control everything with a tight fist. His approach was old-school Italian, but beyond old-school. He was beginning to build up resentments. There was no talking to him anymore; he wouldn't bend an inch. It didn't seem healthy; it wasn't like him. He had always listened and weighed both sides. I remember watching him act this way in conversations with the family.

It was as if he didn't trust anyone anymore after his breakdown and shock treatments—like he couldn't bend at all. It seemed the only one Dad trusted was my mom.

Rita was arguing with our father about her wedding. He was choosing everything . . . even her bridal flowers. She wanted daisies in her bouquet. I remember her saying, "Ma, what is wrong with me wanting to even choose my own flowers? I want daisies in it. Dad thinks there shouldn't be, so I can't have them. I wish I could not have this wedding at all, and just have what I want. I want it small; he has to invite everybody. Ma, he's making me miserable." I felt awful for her. Dad made the florist decide Rita's bouquet. Mr. Rooney really liked Rita, and had to make her something different and special, like she was. She didn't see her bouquet until she opened the box on her wedding day. The corsages were individually wrapped and made into teardrop bouquets with white satin ribbons. I thought it was stunning. It was so unusual. I have never seen anything like it, before or after. I couldn't take my eyes off them—they took my breath away.

Rita absolutely hated it. She had tears in her eyes. I had always liked different, unusual things that made you look twice because of their rare beauty. Rita always liked simple things that spoke for themselves in a more natural way.

The only way I could describe her bouquet was this: when my son Rob got a little older, I decided to get a Christmas tree that was completely different. When he was young, Robert had had real trees every time—I made sure of it. This one belonged out on a lawn. It caught my eye, and it touched my soul. It was just white wires, with white lights at the end of each wire. It had an ethereal look, so spiritual and stunning. I just loved it. One day, Robert sat back looking at it, and after a short while, he said, "Only my mother would buy a Christmas tree on crack." That is what Rita's bridal bouquet looked like. I think my father and Mr. Rooney confused her with me.

Finally, the wedding day came. It was great; I enjoyed every minute of it. Dad had chosen the Waldorf Astoria Hotel. There were 300 people, and everyone I knew there was happy. It would have been my choice in a heartbeat. Nothing Dad chose would have been Rita's choice. She loved Jack like crazy, but that was what Rita was like. She didn't have a mean bone in her body. The photographer caught a picture of her toward the end of the wedding, standing up and looking down at her bouquet on the table before her. She was so sad and disappointed, yet there was an acceptance, too. She understood my father, and knew he thought her so special that he put his whole heart into making her wedding the best he could. My parents had that picture on my father's armoire. I felt sorrowful for her. It seemed that whatever natural joy had been in the family was now gone.

Dad was arguing with Aunt Camy and his mother. Don't ask me specifics, because I was kept out of it. I just got whiffs that they were fighting. The more they argued, the more I was kept in Mill Basin, and Mom wasn't complaining. Apparently, she was angry, too, or just wasn't siding with anyone but my father.

I was slowly losing everything that had made life worth living. Even beautiful Johanna, Joanne's friend, was gone. When she was eighteen, she began getting severe headaches. It was found that she had a brain tumor. It was operated on, and she died. Joanne wouldn't let me go to her funeral. She said she only wanted me to remember Johanna the way she looked before the operation. I would not have recognized her. Her long black hair had been cut off, and her body was all swollen. I wanted to say goodbye to her and pay my respects, but I didn't want to see her mother cry: that would have been devastating. She had loved her beautiful daughter. I knew her heart had been torn from her. I was grateful that my last memory of Johanna was playing with her in front of my grandparents' home in the snow. I still can't imagine what she looked like in the casket, and I will always love Joanne for sparing me that final heartbreak. What I remember most of all were her big, dark-brown, tender, almond-shaped eyes. She is the only person I still cry about over her death. Not all the time, but still, more easily than anyone else. She still touches me.

I was getting concerned about which high school I would be headed to. I had no rudder, and there was no time to help me find out what would be best for me. Aunt Camy wasn't to be listened to anymore, apparently. She suggested Stella Marris. I was so afraid that maybe because she was mad at my dad, she would be mad at me, too, and that she didn't really care anymore. Her choice was perfect, of course; I would have excelled. My parents, on the other hand, thought that since Joanne had excelled at St. Joseph's High School, that meant that I would. I couldn't take ballet classes, because Rita was a klutz. I had to go to a school I never wanted to attend because Joanne had done great there. I was left on the doorstep, so to speak, and it wasn't even my house.

Then Joanne went on a retreat with her class right before graduation. She came back talking a mile a minute, just speeding out of control. I hadn't been spending a lot of time with her, but this didn't seem healthy, either. I felt the old fear grip me again, but after the humiliation I had felt over Dad having a nervous breakdown, I simply had no more strength for watching another. Joanne scared me, and I felt helpless to help her. Me, of all people. It broke my heart to see her suffering the same kind of hell as my dad.

I had felt so secure and loved, but now I felt the ground being pulled out from under my feet, and no one was there to help me. Depression and isolation were starting to set in, but of course, I couldn't show it, because my mom was dealing with a full hand again, and I wasn't going near my dad anymore, at least not for now. I had pretty much given up on being seen or cared for at all anymore, because everyone was going through some kind of crisis. I was just thirteen, which was an awkward time for me. I was still mourning only needing to wear undershirts. Before graduation, however, my school had a dance—the whole graduating class. There would be a band, and it was going to be a time to relax and have fun. I wanted suede fringe boots. They were in style. I loved the feel of suede, and they were just so cool. That was all I remember really wanting to wear: jeans and a sweater were fine with me.

My mom used to buy me stupid-looking stuff, nothing cool, ever. She would insist on buying it. I would tell her, "I don't like it. I am not wearing it." She said I "would look so pretty in it." Pink ruffled stuff that was never really me. If I did get something like that, it had to be something I felt really comfortable in—nothing that buttoned to the neck, strangling me with a ruffle. We would go back and forth. After giving up I would say, "Okay, Ma. Go ahead buy it." I kept it all in the closet, and never wore it. There was no way in hell was I ever going to wear any of it.

After about two or three shopping trips like this, she finally got that it was what I was comfortable in, not what she thought I would look "pretty in." She loved those words. I liked a classic look, when it came down to it. When she understood what I was doing with the clothes, she wouldn't take me shopping anymore. I had to ask my father for money to buy my clothes, and I went alone.

When it came to this dance, I told my father all I wanted were these boots. He said, "No."

I lost it. *Come on already, I am done with this stuff.* I told him, "No problem, if I can't wear what I want, I just won't go to the dance." I wanted to say, "So what? It wasn't like I ever did anything with my classmates anyway, why should this be different? I could live without going."

When he saw I meant it and I turned to leave, he called me back. "Laura," he said. "Everyone will be wearing jeans and boots. Why should you? You should wear a dress. Men like and respect women who dress nicely, who wear something they look really good in, that complements them."

I said, "Dad, a dress?"

"I will give you money, and you find something you like."

Compromise. I can compromise very well if it makes sense, and the compromise makes both parties happy. I said, "Okay. If I don't find anything I like, I won't go to the dance, and I don't care."

I left the house for a shopping trip without my mother for the first time, and went to a local store that had more modern clothes. I knew what looked good on women, because I saw how my aunt and cousin and sister looked. Looking good wasn't a problem for them, so . . . I looked through the racks and saw this deep blue dress with a V-neck. It had a soft white leather band on the entire V of the neck, a white leather band at the cuffs, and white leather at the hem, with a soft white leather belt. It was beautiful, and a perfect compromise. I might have bought white shoes, too—I don't remember.

I wore my hair down. It was my only feature I felt any pride in. It was really pretty. I wore a little bit of make-up. Even now, I never wear a lot of make-up; I don't like the feel of it. When I got dressed and showed my dad, he said, "That is what I meant." He was just as pleased with my choice as I was. I could have cried, because he took the time to teach me like he had taught Rita.

I felt so pretty, but also cautious as I walked into the dance. I had walked there alone, and it felt great. I might have felt good about my appearance in the house, but I didn't know how accepted I would be by my classmates. They had only seen me in my uniform.

Only Jimmy Ryan from across the street had ever seen me out of it. I held my breath and walked in.

I didn't get a bad response at all, considering that I was the only one in a nice dress. I couldn't believe it—a guy in the band who wasn't from the neighborhood, but had to travel to get there, really liked me. I mean, liked me enough to write to me a number of times, and even sent me a really pretty delicate necklace in the mail. I was in shock, and embarrassed about that. I had gotten way more attention than I was prepared for.

In half an hour, my father had taught me a lesson that would last a lifetime. In other words, it didn't matter who the woman was, it was how a woman took care of herself if she wanted to be taken seriously. Any woman could be beautiful. Of course, he said it didn't always have to cost a lot. He didn't give me a lot of money—just enough for what I needed, to the penny. That was why I loved my dad. This was who he was. He taught me life lessons intelligently, gently, and honestly . . . lessons he never had to teach me again. Once was enough. That was the last time I felt he really saw me and loved me just the way I was. It was the last time he had the time for me.

Of course, that was before we came to know each other as adults. In the end, it came down to the fact that I didn't like Daffy Duck—he annoyed me to no end. Dad didn't like Bugs Bunny . . . thought he was a real smart ass. We agreed to intelligently disagree about who was more annoying and still love each other, even though at heart he was just an annoying duck, and I was a smart-ass bunny.

It was a long road before I became an adult, though—a long, rocky, painful road. Rita was happy she was out of the house, and happy to have her own life with Jack in Queens, far from Brooklyn and the old neighborhoods. She had gotten a fresh start and I missed her big time, but I was happy for her. Her happiness was the only joy left to me anymore. She was the part of my family that was not going to hell.

Joanne and I graduated on the same day. I had gotten into two out of three high schools, and was on the waiting list for the third. All Catholic, of course. I didn't feel so stupid; but I was beginning to believe I couldn't reach my full potential, intellectually or emotionally, no matter how hard I tried. I was being fractured. Come that summer, I was shipped off to Uncle Benny's, but right before I left, Grandpa was back in the hospital for the umpteenth time. He always came back home. Mom said to me, "Grandpa wants to see you."

I said, "Next time. I just don't feel like going." She failed to explain to me that it would be the last time I would ever see him again. For some reason, my family always saw me as older than I was, and it was assumed that I knew what was happening. I went to my Uncle Benny's; I think he picked me up. I don't really remember. It felt like heaven being there again: fresh air, no family arguing, away from the heavy blanket of sickness. They didn't tell me Grandpa had leukemia. I found out after he died. I think they knew it would have sunk in, and they didn't want any more grief before the shit hit the fan.

It was not a long time, I think just days after I got to Uncle Benny's, that my uncle said, "Get ready, we are going fishing." I didn't want to go. I wanted to stay close to home. He insisted. For the first time, while preparing to go, I had a deeply spiritual experience. I felt, saw, and heard Mary, Mother of Jesus, say to me, "Don't worry, he is all right." It took me a minute to realize what had happened. It was as if time had stopped for as long as it took for the words to be spoken. Just long enough to feel the truth of what was being said to me. Then it struck me: Grandpa had died. I told Uncle Benny, "I want to go home." He said, "We are going fishing." He knew that always brought fun; but I also knew I should be on my way home, not fishing. There was no way we weren't going fishing. Within half an hour, I got so seasick I couldn't bear it. The last thing I remember on the boat was talking with JoJo about how bad I was feeling. I had never gotten seasick before. I was watching Peter and listening to the boys talking. Then, when we finally got back to Uncle Benny's house and the fish were taken care of, I was told to pack. He was taking me home. Then it was waiting, just watching what was going to happen.

I was good with Grandpa, and at peace. I knew where he was. The fact that I had never once seen him going to church, except for a funeral, didn't matter at all. It was as if the fresh rose Grandma kept in front of Mary's statue every week, and her prayers, served as a reminder that Our Lady had stayed close to him and loved him, and watched him while he slept. He was loved just as he was, and my curiosity about where he had gone was satisfied.

I did wish I had gone to see him when he wanted to see me. I felt terrible; it broke my heart. I loved him, and it was a terrible thing to keep from him . . . his little granddaughter he would give a horsey ride on his knee until it hurt his old joints. I was fine every time he said he had to stop. I will never forget the laughs we shared as I held onto him for dear life, nearly bounced off as if it were a real horse. He was the only one who would get me banana splits, because they were so expensive. He gave me money to help heal children with leukemia every time I asked. He never held back once. I never forgot that he told me before he died not to become a funeral director. He knew me, and loved me just the way I was, and it was okay with him. I loved being creative more than anything. He watched me closer even than Aunt Camy.

CHAPTER 9

Becoming a Young Woman

GRANDPA'S FUNERAL wasn't a high point for our family. It was a pivotal one, just like turning thirteen had been for me. When Uncle Benny made the left-hand turn from Court Street onto Dean Street when he went to park, I was gearing up to get out of the car. I looked up and saw that the whole front of the funeral home, from the Dean Street corner, was filled with people in black: talking, smoking, standing alone in thought. My first thought was, *another large funeral.* Then I got out of the car, and had to wait until Uncle Benny said it was okay to cross the street, which was both funny and annoying. Traffic was something to play chicken with in Brooklyn. You knew if you lived near a busy street, it is just a matter of timing and the ability to assess the situation quickly. I gave in to Uncle Benny, and waited to cross the street with him. It was something I just had to do. I loved him, and had to respect him. I realized he loved me, and didn't want anything to hurt me. He was strong and gentle with me, but it pissed me off nonetheless. At the same time, it kind of gave me a moment to decide whether or not I wanted to cross the street. I thought they would have called me home as soon as Grandpa died, and I would be home before he was embalmed and the wake started—the usual routine for everyone. I thought I would have been respected that much, that I would be a part of his funeral with him from beginning to end. I didn't want to know anything different.

We crossed the street, rang the bell, waited to be buzzed in, and started up the stairs. The minute I got to the top, the bell rang again. I happened to be the closest to the buzzer, so I buzzed the door open and called down, "Who is it?" As I turned out of the foyer back to the steps to look over the railing, I saw it was Marie, dressed in all black from head to shoes. She said, "I am going to buy some new stockings."

I said, "Okay," and she turned and left. My heart sunk. I didn't want to see that the wake was already going on, or that I had missed so much of it. I had to face the fact that what was happening was real: Grandpa was dead. At the same moment, I realized this was another reason I didn't want to get older. But I couldn't go back, no matter how much I wanted to. I had to steady myself and go forward. But something in me begged to go back.

When I turned and walked into the kitchen, I was not told that Grandpa had died by anyone. It was assumed that I knew. Everyone was in black from head to toe. I felt numb. The grief after the death of a loved one visited us in our home that day. It was just a hard, cold reality. Pain, shock, grief, you name it . . . it was not happening to someone else. It was a punch in the stomach that knocked the wind out of me. This time, it had happened to all of my family and friends. I had to steel myself against knowing that I was older and would be overlooked, no matter how it much it hurt. I was old enough to handle it myself now, alone.

Instantly, I was thrown. I took in the common experience of the weight of that piece of you that dies with a person. For a time, you die, too, and are with them. Another emptiness of life became apparent in that moment. Where life as you know it, where you wholly fit in, is transformed into a different world. It is an uncomfortable and painful adjustment . . . perhaps for the rest of your life. A part of you is still with them, but they are not there. There is only the wanting for the space they held to be filled with them once more.

I needed to be quiet, and just wanted to be with him, even just to be close to his body, even knowing there would be no warmth emanating from it. It was a crushing experience, knowing that Grandpa was out of my hands. It shattered my world. No more watching him tear the plastic wrap off that DiNobili cigar of his, gagging when he lit it, and making the decision if I should go with him when he bought them, knowing that if I didn't, we would both be less for missing the experience of being together.

There were just too many people around me. It was too busy for me to process what people in my family and at the wake were experiencing individually—the other people I knew who loved Grandpa/Al/BoBo, too.

Years later, I found out that to my grandmother's chagrin, Grandpa's girlfriend loved him a little too much, too. Mom said to me in a whisper, "Grandpa's girlfriend showed up at the funeral. Grandma was furious." Like my mom said, in an Italian family at the time, if a man didn't have a girlfriend and he was of the ilk, he wasn't a man—a real catch-22 for women (as if now is any different). I can tell you, having another woman on the side doesn't make your "bride" very happy—bottom line. Especially when she was not the one to take on a lover first.

I was only aware that my mom nodded her head to me and said, "Come on, we will get you some clothes." That meant black stockings, like Marie needed. It was the only thing that clearly registered at that moment: clothes. I wasn't a little girl anymore. I was an adolescent of thirteen, old enough to know I would have to deal with it on my own.

I didn't want to leave. I wanted to go immediately across the street and be with Grandpa, but I had to realize that I was going to a funeral, and there were things that had to be done. Like it or not, it was a social experience; I couldn't be alone with him, even for a private moment like I'd had with Bobby. There was no time just to be with him and only him in *any* moment anymore. I had no time to become angry at that. I had to shove it down and know it would just have to wait to be dealt with. I knew that somewhere in me, there was anger. Some of it passed by, like seeing something out of the corner of my eye. I wasn't quite sure exactly why that touch of anger was there. It was too much to process all at once when there was so much traffic surrounding me.

The thing is, I never felt angry over his death, and still don't. I know he is in a peaceful place. Grandpa was human, and knowing he was all right kept me from feeling completely cut off from him. That split second of knowing has kept a small line, maybe the width of a string, of acceptance and quietude of spirit that exists in me to this day. If I can balance and walk on that string there lies in the smile between us, there is no void; there is still warmth. Today, I have an understanding, and still, a deep love for Grandpa exists.

There is only one thing I have experienced every painful thought and emotion over: the fact that I didn't go to the hospital to see him when he asked, and it was for the last time, too. It also happened to be the only thing he ever really asked of me.

Learning to be a humane human being is a lifetime job, and there is no better one. There are times when things seem to get in the way, or there isn't enough time. I have noticed that some people do become humane very quickly, but then there is not enough time because they pass on unexpectedly—too soon or too young.

Not granting Grandpa his last request remains a sorrow for me now, but there is no more anger, no more of my mind and emotions darting with lightning strikes aimed at the lightning rod of my heart every time. Only fifty years had to pass in order to accept it to the point of pure sorrow. That's how deep and painful that first realization was of what I had done. They call it eating an elephant by yourself, one bite at a time. For a child, a bull elephant isn't an easy thing to eat. Just developing a taste for it can take a long time. I know with assuredness: it was for me, even though it was never explained to me how sick he was.

One good thing happened at the funeral, though. There was a couple who owned the pharmacy across the street, and on the walls were shelves of knick-knacks to buy. The wife told me one day that Grandpa had asked her if she was "interested in some underground novelties." Grandpa had a sense of humor.

Within the three days of his wake, it seemed like hundreds of people were there. I know there were three flower cars needed, and flower pieces were in his hearse, also. I was numb and guilt-ridden about taking that dime out of St. Jude's fountain to see how Kotex would come out of that machine. Maybe it wouldn't have been so bad if he hadn't died of leukemia. Granted, he wasn't a child; but he had died from the same thing. That dime could have gone toward research for the cure. Now I know at this time eighty percent of children with leukemia are cured, and no matter what happens, I had a part in it. Research is still going on, and I am still donating.

When the wake ended, we went to the funeral Mass across the street, a block down Court Street. Flowers were brought to the front of the church. There were so many, one of the pallbearers had to move the large candle so there would be more room for the casket. The wax from the candle poured over his shoulder. He said he was okay, but now, looking back, it was like a preview of the way my family, in making room for Grandpa's death, would be poured out like hot wax.

I remember it rained for a month after his funeral. He died in the second week of July. There was a lot of talk about it around the kitchen table, and how in the Bible, it had rained for forty days. *Good*, I thought, *something about the Bible; maybe peace will reign in the house.* I never thought it through that when it rained for forty days, the flood destroyed everything.

As time passed, there were more out-and-out verbal fights downtown. I didn't know it was about money. One day, a bad verbal fight broke out between my dad and Aunt Camy. It was a whopper. Aunt Camy said something about him acting crazy, and she was going to call the cops. He pulled the phone off the wall. I hid in the bedroom attached to the kitchen. Mom gathered me and everything up and said, "Leo, let's go home. Now!" Somehow, he heard her, and I was driven home. I don't know where Joanne was that day; she was still living there.

That was it. I never went there again. The last time I saw it, it was the only building in the area that looked gutted of anything that is loving. It needed repairs, was painted in an ugly way, and contained a dive bar. I felt sick when I looked at it.

CHAPTER 10

Plays and Characters

Two things happened before my last trip through my grandparents' front door. First, Marie saw me. It was the second or third time that her love for me touched me so deeply, it kept my head above water—the will to live a happy life and stay alive.

One night, amid all the turmoil in the house, she said to me, "Laura? Would you like to meet me for lunch in the city?" I couldn't believe my ears. Not only did she see me, but she was willing to take me into her world of work on Wall Street. Smart, professional men and women worked in big corporate offices there, and the historic value in itself made me forget the world of pain and isolation and loss. I was in for that. "You bet," I said.

She told me which train to take, and where to meet her. It was only a few short train stops away—not difficult to get to, but if you know the area, it is a maze of streets crossing and intersecting. Of course, I got lost. I found her anyway, and I was going to act like, *Me, get lost? No, that was too simple a set of directions to get lost from.* I was sweating from walking really fast up and down the streets to find the place. When I saw her, relief covered me. Marie said, "You got off the wrong end of the train. I figured you might have when I didn't see you." I groaned. I was hoping she hadn't noticed.

"There is a nice place to eat near here," said Marie. "Let's hurry, I have to get back to work."

"Okay," I said, and stayed as close to her as I could get. I was not at all familiar with this maze of streets, and loads of people were walking in every direction. Such a large, steady flow of people: going up the street, going down the street, crossing the streets, and people going in and out of buildings with people waiting outside, mostly dressed in suits and nice clothes.

I wanted to take it all in, but we had to rush if we wanted to enjoy lunch without having to eat it very fast. I don't remember where we stopped. I don't even remember walking into the restaurant, except being seated at a table with a very clean white tablecloth. The place was very nice, as a matter of fact. I was surprised she cared about me enough to take me to such an adult restaurant.

The waiter came over and handed us our menu. It was so big, I had trouble even making out where to start. Marie said, "I'll order for us." I kept quiet, and kind of held my breath. I didn't know if she knew what I liked, and the atmosphere was so different, I didn't know what I would end up eating. She ordered a hot open roast beef sandwich with gravy for me. I don't remember what was on the rest of the plate; most likely, hot, buttered mashed potatoes and a vegetable. She had ordered a Coke for me while we waited, which had already put me over the top. I had never seen a straw in a glass of Coke with the paper still on it halfway up. I couldn't figure out why they would do that. Then I realized it kept it clean where I would be drinking from it. Very chic.

I looked at Marie, and gave her a big smile and an unspoken thank-you. I was so happy. She knew it, too, and like Aunt Camy, she gave me a look that said *not to worry*. Marie was quiet. We didn't talk much, but sat quietly and ate. Rita and I would have found it difficult to remain so quiet. It wasn't in our nature when we were together. We would always end up laughing.

I completely decompressed. I was overjoyed, taking it all in with her. I had never had that kind of sandwich before, and it is still one of my favorites. Every time I have one, I take time while looking at the plate to say a silent, happy thank-you to Marie. I would have never known anything about their existence had it not been for her that day. This always makes them taste even better, even if they aren't made that well (at a diner, for example). The taste of that memory makes it worth ordering. I don't even remember if we had any dessert, like ice cream.

The memory that grooved itself in me was feeling like a composed true New Yorker acting in accordance with the environment. And Marie saying, "It's getting late, I have to get back to work. I'll take you to the train where you will get off closer to home." I was a bit embarrassed, because I was reminded of my goof. I came to find out later on that the part of my brain that lights up where direction is involved only lights up to the wattage of a nightlight behind a table.

I gave Marie a kiss on the cheek, and thanked her with all my heart. All that sadness and not knowing what was going to happen to me vanished, and room was made in me for hope: that I would grow up to be a mature adult, who knew that a quiet existed in me no matter how much noise surrounded me. Marie had developed a future in New York for me with respect.

Things were reaching more of a fevered pitch in the house. I was missing Grandpa, and the grounding I had known was being blown out of the water. At one time, I had known I was going to get married young, love my husband, be loved, and have three children. I wanted three children. While I was trying to figure out how I was going to do that with all the anger around me again, Marie broke the trance. She said to me, "Laura, would you like to see a play with me?" She stopped me in my tracks. I was speechless. "Yes," I finally responded.

It wasn't long before we were on our way to Manhattan in our best attire. The play was *Plaza Suite*. I couldn't figure out why she would take me to a play that was so mature. I couldn't really enjoy the subject, but Shelly Winters was in it, and I had seen her a lot in movies. I watched her live on stage with wide eyes. I didn't know this is what the city held. I was hooked. I had become a dyed-in-the-wool New Yorker.

As a footnote, my son Rob loved my father, and a big hole was left in his heart when he passed away when Rob was twelve. I asked Rob if he would like to see a play, and he said yes. I made sure to let him pick out the play. He chose *Dr. Jekyll and Mr. Hyde*, which would not have been my choice, but it hit the spot for a twelve-year-old boy. It was awesome! The star of the show couldn't be there, so the understudy performed. I made Rob wait until the end, and the understudy came out the stage door. I had Robert talk with him about acting and what they had in common, just as guys. Of course, it embarrassed him, but I didn't care; he would remember it, and it propelled him out of grief for a few hours. That was when he, too, began to learn to be a true New Yorker. I also took him to see the Rockettes that Christmas. His jaw dropped. Let's just say he loved it, and thoroughly enjoyed it. It was colorful and beautiful, and the whole production was just so classy. Those women were truly talented dancers. They did well in sparkling, skimpy-looking clothes, especially as reindeer.

By the time I was thirteen, though, all the fun had ended. Nobody was speaking to anyone. Worst of all, I didn't know where I had been tied into the family knot being pulled from each side. I just got more depressed, and geared myself up for a high school I didn't want to attend.

CHAPTER 11

A Stroke Isn't Necessarily What You Do to Your Cat, nor Does It Have to Do with Luck

ONE NIGHT, right before high school started, my dad was working late. Mom used to let me sleep in her bed sometimes because there was a TV in their room. I loved watching Steve Allen. He was the only late-night talk show host who could make me fall out of bed laughing. I must have kept the TV on—all I knew was that I had fallen asleep in my parents' bed, which never really happened. I always ended up in my bed. I think this was the only time I actually slept there all night. I woke up really early, realized where I was, and knew I should get back into my bed after going to the bathroom. As I was headed there, I nearly tripped over my dad on the floor. I lost my breath. I knelt down on the floor and asked, "Dad, are you all right?"

He was completely confused and paralyzed. I don't remember if I ran to my mom or yelled out for her. I kind of went into shock. I know my mom called Rita and the ambulance. Rita was about half an hour away by car. Mom called a friend to come over and watch me, even though Joanne was there—though I don't remember her being around that night, or showing up at all. There were so many people, and I remember my mom washing some dishes. I looked at her and wondered, *Why would she be doing dishes?* They say women commit suicide with pills so they won't leave a mess. In my experience, women just clean up when they freak out, perhaps to bring order into chaos. My mom didn't want me to be alone, I guess, if Joanne had to go to the hospital, too.

The ambulance came. Rita was there, and my dad's friend Joe. Mom, Rita, and Dad went to the hospital. Joe stayed with us. I wished his wife was there. She was so kind and gentle—like another mom, but a friend-mom. All I knew was, her husband scared me; he just seemed a little too slimy for my taste. He was big and loud, and spit when he talked. I avoided him as much as possible. There had been so much chaos that morning, which made me even more upset that I wasn't allowed to go to the hospital. My head was spinning. I stayed in the kitchen, hoping to avoid Joe. Something just wasn't right with that guy. I just didn't trust him.

Joanne was in our bedroom. I remember she was sitting on the bed crying, and he went into the bedroom. I wanted to scream and tell him to leave, that he didn't have to be there. I didn't know what to do.

Joanne was alone in there with him, and he was sitting too close to her. I looked in, and saw he was all over her. He was running his hand from her shoulder down over her breast. She got even more upset, and pushed him out and made him leave. That was it. I couldn't believe what was happening. It was if my mind had broken. I later learned that I had experienced an anxiety attack.

Dad's stroke left him paralyzed on his whole right side. I think that put Joanne over the edge, too. Afterward, she was hospitalized for the first time for an emotional and psychological collapse.

CHAPTER 12

High School

Every day, I had to travel for an hour on the bus and train to get downtown, then back again, rather than just walking to my grandparents' house, which Joanne had the luxury of doing. Every day, I hated it more and more. It was painful. I was picked on by this Italian girl in my class, Regina, who was known as an "Italian hitter." An Italian hitter is someone known for their street fights, who may also be known to pull a knife as part of a neighborhood gang. Just like in the movies. She had black hair and black eyelashes, would roll her uniform skirt up to her wazoo, and wore a leather jacket. She hung out at the corner candy store, smoked, and was small, so she had to make up for it with her toughness. That was probably why her parents put her in a Catholic school—hoping it might civilize her. She saw I was weak and didn't fit in, so she hated me. She was a bully and I was her victim, or so she thought. She made fun of me and kept me more uncomfortable than I could already bear just being there, and I wasn't too thrilled with her, either.

One day, she cornered me with some girls, and said, "I'm going to put you in one of your father's caskets." I wanted to know which one she would choose. And since she would be purchasing one from my father's caskets, that scared me. I had never been targeted before. I told my dad what she said. After he had stopped laughing, and with his impaired speech, he spoke to the principal. Regina never chose which casket she was going to use. I had her and the whole threat thing buried nice and swiftly. She was dead meat, and never bothered me again. I got chewed out by the principal, who told me after pulling me into her office that day, "You got your father involved in this, and he is a sick man. How selfish can you be?" I just hated it there.

It was Christmas vacation, and my homeroom teacher was this calcified old nun. She looked like she needed to drink Pennzoil instead of orange juice in the morning just to walk. She told us, "It is Christmas. Why don't you get involved with your church at home and do some community service?" I was so miserable, I thought it might be a good idea. My church was putting together a caroling choir to sing through the neighborhood. I thought, *Oh, great! This, at least, should be fun.* We gathered together and started visiting houses in the neighborhood. I got so into it, I started singing my heart out. For this, I was told, "Stop it. I don't think it is right for you to sing so badly just for fun. You're ruining it for everyone!" I shut my mouth, and didn't sing again all evening.

God heard my misery that night. The church across the street had invited a professional choir leader and full professional band to come for a Christmas concert. I joined it. I actually joined the choir, figuring I might learn to sing. I did well, and was put in the center of the choir. One of the places we sang was at Carnegie Hall. God is good. A nice Christmas gift, no? They started to rack up.

I was pretty much at the end of my rope, however, at St. Joseph's High School. One day, a classmate named Daisy didn't do her math homework one night, and she knew she was going to get screwed by the teacher for it. I loved her name, but she hated it: "It's embarrassing," she told me. She was this beautiful auburn-haired Spanish girl who dyed her hair. It looked wonderful with her complexion, and made her look much older than her age. I gave her my homework to copy. I got caught, and was chewed out about being so irresponsible in front of everyone. That was it—I snapped.

I stood up straight and started singing—out loud—an old song about being irresponsible and having it being undeniably true. The teacher looked at me in shock and just walked away. I passed that class by the skin of my teeth, only because I loved algebra, and did well in it. The nun went into a cloister at the end of the year.

I joined the school's bowling league just to break the routine of wanting to kill myself. Cathy Carroll, with whom I had gone to grammar school, went to St.

Joe's, also. She lived close to my block at home. She wasn't in my class, but we decided to join the league together. We were both miserable at St. Joseph's, and figured we had some history together. We were friends, and we thought some fun and laughter might make the hell we were in more enjoyable. I think we went three times. We had so much fun, even though we were lousy bowlers. She might have been a touch better than me. It was hysterical—we were so bad, and were trying to do so well. The head of the league came over and yelled at us because we were ruining the league's standing. We left.

The school year was ending, and I found out that my cousin Janet was going to a hairdressing school one block away. Our schedules were different, but it was comforting to know she was nearby. At least I had one friend and one family member in my life downtown now. I continued limping along.

We took our final class trip to Riis Park, and took a boat to get there. I had never really smoked—yes, at Aunt Helen's, but not enough to become full-blown addicted to the things. On this boat ride, I got the chance to relax and look at where I was in my life. I smoked a pack and a half that day, and didn't stop until I was up to three packs a day, twenty-five years later. It was Rita's death years later from lung cancer that made me stop. Seeing her with tubes up her back, then being stitched up with a baseball stitch I had learned to do at the morgue was enough for me. I wasn't going to have Robert see me die like that if I could help it. Because baseball was Rita's life, it was *apropos* for a life on life's terms. Certainly not always fun and games.

On the last day of school at St. Joseph's High School, I got my report card. I was being thrown out. I knew that was not going to go well with my father. He had developed, by this time, a mean anger at life. Something had broken in his brain. Even his speech was affected; all he could do was curse. The doctor said it had affected that area of his brain.

I happened to have met Janet that day walking to the train station. She saw how miserable I was. She cut her classes to go home with me so I wouldn't be alone when I had to face my father. She knew things were not going to go over well at all. Family was still family; it wasn't all bad, all the time. Janet came upstairs with me. We agreed that maybe he wouldn't take it really badly if she was there. He knew I was coming home with the report card, and wanted to see it pretty much as soon as I walked in. I think he had it in mind that I was Joanne, and was going to bring him all As so he could take pride in something that made him feel good.

We know that didn't happen. When he saw it, he had to read it three times to register that I had failed practically everything, and was being thrown out. He started getting really mad, and told Janet to go get her hair scissors. My hair was the only thing that made me feel good about myself. It was still long and pretty, and it was a comfort to play with if I was thinking or just wanted to touch it. It always comforted me. When I was little, my mom had to lay next to me so I could curl her hair with my finger in order to sleep. Once, she told me I forced my dad to lay next to me so I could curl his hair, and he did. His hair was short, so it didn't curl around my finger, but it didn't matter—it still put me to sleep. I didn't suck my thumb; I played with hair.

Well, Janet didn't want to get her scissors. My father was getting so furious, she got scared, and went and got them. He made me sit in front of him at the kitchen table, and said to Janet, "Cut her hair." It just hollowed me out. I wasn't going to give him the satisfaction of thinking that what he was doing was right by me—either going to St. Joseph's or cutting my hair. I stared him down, and didn't cry. The more I did that, the more he told Janet to cut it shorter. I think Janet was crying. Finally, it was about two inches long. I got up and walked away, and didn't care if he never spoke to me again. He could ignore me for the rest of his life, and I would be grateful. One of Janet's friends told me I looked like a carrot with my hair sticking up like that. I just took it, and my heart started steeling up cold. I began wondering where my buddy God had gone. He didn't seem to be anywhere around.

CHAPTER 13

When Change Changes—
Not on Purpose, but by Desire

AFTER THE DISASTER of my first year of Catholic High School, I had to go to summer school: Erasmus High School, Barbra Streisand's alma mater. It was beginning to look dilapidated by the time I got there. Erasmus had a huge campus built of stone bricks. I fell in love with it, but if I'd had my druthers, I would have put about a million dollars into repairs.

It was there that I fell into my element. The pace was more relaxed, and the teachers were, too. This was conducive to my type of learning, and my weeks weren't being disturbed by all the travel and change of environment. An environment with an overload of information that requires children to sit and concentrate on schoolwork did not work for me as it does for others. I imagine this may be what children of divorce experience: same family, but different houses and lives in the span of a week. Being highly sensitive did not make it any easier for me in terms of schoolwork. Highly sensitive people need a lot of alone time to process information.

I need absolute isolation to study or work in order to give it my full attention and do well. Otherwise, the glut of information around me feels like the constant scraping of nails on a chalkboard. It makes me very cranky. Ask my son. It feels to me like an iron spoon beating the inside of a metal pot next to my ear while I'm sleeping early on Sunday morning and being told to "Get up, I am wasting the day." I believe Uncle Jimmy caused nerve damage that way, and not just once. He enjoyed it. In my opinion, he was purely annoying and a jerk.

And I am sorry for anyone within ten yards of me when I need to concentrate and give something my full attention. I loved being married; I love being alone. Alone works best for me the older I get. My creativity is at full throttle again. That doesn't mean I don't talk to friends every day. I do.

That summer, I was left alone enough to enjoy the stability of a steady routine. Just enough travel to enjoy it before it got tedious. A grand, beautiful school (with potential—I felt like I belonged there) in a historic area with shopping. Not everyone wanted to be there in the summer, but it fed my soul. It made it easier to avoid the disturbance still going on in my family. I wasn't dependent on anyone to keep me away from it. It was as easy as sitting in the backyard or on the stoop. I could close my door to study or find a quiet place with only a few people instead of nine. My dad was purposely avoiding me, anyway. That was welcome. I was free. I passed my classes easily, was sorry when it ended, and enjoyed the rest of the summer before the second year of high school was upon me.

A brand-new high school, South Shore, had opened about a mile away. I loved to walk there. It was a ten- or fifteen-minute bus ride away or a half-hour walk, if I took my time and enjoyed it. Mom took responsibility for all the work to transfer me to South Shore. It was brand spanking new; not even finished yet. There was a beautiful rotunda in the front, and I felt the anticipation of attending classes in it. I was nervous, but my cousin Rose, Janet's eldest sister, had a friend who taught there: Mr. Klein. He worked in the program office, and I happened to meet him when I went to visit. He asked me if I wanted to work in the program office, too. I told him I would give it thought. I eventually decided to do it; he was a cheery, nice guy. I would wait until I had settled in. He knew what the place looked like inside; I didn't, yet.

Around that time, Rose said something to me that changed my life forever. She asked me, "What's the most important word in the English language?" I may be paraphrasing her question, but that sums it up.

I said, "I don't know."

"Communication," she responded. This flung open the doors of my mind to a new way of being. I didn't have to think; her statement had hit its mark.

I felt grounded for the first time in my life. I was putting roots down, and even had the potential for a job that would allow me to help make the school work and flow. It was awkward, at first, being there. I would be living full-time in one home for the first time. I was a steady part of the neighborhood now, and there was no avoiding allowing the neighbors to get to know me. How could I explain the part of my life they didn't know about? *I might meet my old classmates*, I thought.

But it was all new to everyone. It was a big school. People got lost easily. Parts of the place were still under construction, and you had to go around them to get to class. I began to feel a bit out of place after I got my schedule . . . lonely. I decided that since I had a better idea than God about what was good for me, I would keep God on the sidelines and take charge of my own life, not Him. *He didn't do a good job when I needed it*, I thought. I had turned fourteen at St. Joseph's, and was still fourteen at South Shore, but on the brink of fifteen—awkward in itself. I did what I knew would ground me: work, making an impact, and letting myself be a child with a brain that wouldn't be fully developed for another ten years or so. I went about directing my life at full steam, without any help from anyone. People and God just seemed too damned painful. It wasn't the smartest thing I ever did, but I did what I did, and God writes in crooked lines.

I found Mr. Klein, and took him up on the offer of working in the program office. I became a part of the school. A necessary part. I was beginning to fit into my own skin. I not only did well in my classes, but knew I had to go to summer school to make up for flunking out the year before. That was fine with me. I was looking forward to it.

When I was home, I either did homework or allowed my creativity full range. I continued taking piano lessons with the reluctance of eating poison. The thing was, I loved playing the piano more than anything, if I was not forced to. No matter how much I tried, I couldn't get Mrs. Boyce to give me a piece of music I wanted to play. I gritted my teeth and forced myself to learn this beautiful instrument, but only because it was a beautiful instrument. It felt like I was dealing with a wily snake that I couldn't get hold of, and it had a painful bite. Hours of practicing music I could have learned in a third of the time, had I liked what I was playing. I would have loved even doing the scales to build strength and dexterity. An instrument is a gift from God. It should never be abused.

One day, my father had a friend over for dinner. Of course, parents do the parent thing and take special care to humiliate you every chance they get. They started talking about the piano.

"Laura, go play the piano," ordered my father—nicely, of course. I said no, but that meant nothing, and had no effect. So off I went to the piano, found the piece of music I hated the least, and played it. I might have been forced to play more than one song, too. I finished, and went back to the table to finish dessert. The man must have been talking about me with Dad. I sat down and looked at the guy with a silent *You happy, now that you heard me play?* He looked at me and smiled, turned to my father and said, "If she were my daughter, I would chain her to that piano." My dad must have mentioned that I didn't like practicing it. I looked back at the man with the thought of taking that chain he was talking about, wrapping it around his mouth, and hanging him in the living room doorway, watching him swing while I played the piano.

I made some excuse, and left the table. If I never saw that guy again, it would be fine with me. Dad was not in the habit of racking up points with me during that time period. If he was going to take that guy's advice, I would have stopped playing, and there would be nothing he could do about it. I would go to the lessons, just sit there, and refuse to play one note. That would have won the battle *and* the war in one stroke. If I came out bloody, well, that's what happens in war. So what?

My mother once told me, "Laura, if you don't stop behaving that way, you are going to be punished and have a child just like yourself." Oh, God, how I wish I had heeded her advice. Always heed your mother's advice; there is some kind of voodoo behind it.

I started drawing, embroidering, doing needlepoint, knitting, crocheting, and cooking. On Thanksgiving, I made a pumpkin pie, took the extra crust, and made a scene with clouds plus a turkey and a bunny running under a tree. It just made my mom laugh that I would even think of doing something like that. Actually, the family just thought it was cool. Mom and I were pretty good friends; she let me express myself without too much grief. I guess she was used to Rita. At least I never did a chemistry experiment on the stove that ended up on the ceiling, walls, and windows like Rita did. I was making my own cards for Christmas and birthdays, and wrapping gifts creatively and precisely with much love and care. I just explored anything and everything that was creative. I had never been so happy.

I started to practice the piano less. My parents thought it was out of spite because they wanted me to play so much, but it wasn't. It was their lack of caring enough to hear what I was saying and do something about it. My mother couldn't hear me; she had wanted to learn the piano with all her heart as a child, and couldn't. Any kind of music to her was right. I think I remember her saying to me once that her family had had a piano when she was a child, and she could play it by ear, but they had to burn it for heat. It was something like that, because it broke her heart, and mine to boot. The story was too hard for me to hear more than once. I wish I could deny ever hearing her saying that. My father, on the other hand, just had to be right, and there was no approaching him. Somewhere, something was broken in him.

The only thing I flunked was geometry. It never clicked for me. I flunked it five times, even in summer school. I would get fours and sevens on the Regents Exams. In my last semester of school, they gave up and let me take a logic class. I never aced anything so quickly. There would be tests that everyone failed so badly the teacher had to grade them on a curve. I ended up getting a hundred and four on one, and a hundred and twelve on another. I never knew that was even possible. I never felt stupid in that class, or that I was a thorough disappointment because I was not using my potential. It was just fun. The teacher used Sherlock Holmes stories for homework as an example of logic. He used an example of a pool table: how the balls hit, and the directions they would go. It was a very fun and useful class. A good teacher can go a long way in a child's life.

I finally understood geometry in my forties, when I took a math level-five class that pushed me past my limits in college. One day on a staircase, I ran into my class advisor, who happened to be a priest, when I was having a bad math day. I grabbed him by the arm and said, "What is wrong with you? Why did you make me take that math class?"

"Because I knew you could do it," he answered.

"Oh." I headed back to tutoring before the class. I finally came to an understanding of geometry, its history, its uses, and how it fit into the universe. Fractals were added to the mix, and one day, while entering class, I put two and two together. I became very quiet, and suddenly realized the "music of the spheres" actually exists. It can be heard. I heard it in that moment.

When I learned later on about string theory and the strings actually vibrating in color, no one could ever tell me what I heard didn't exist. It was perfect, crystal-clear harmony, a concert you could become and be a part of. A perfect communication. Physicists like to explain it as an "elegant universe." Of course, I spent more time in tutoring than in class. It may have been a two-to-one ratio, but it was worth it.

One day, in a class full of eighteen- and twenty-year-olds doing this stuff at lightning speed, I suddenly felt frozen in place. While I was making a tree out of fractals, I said out loud, "I need crayons to color in my tree. Anybody have crayons?" I don't know why that was ignored. I was desperate for crayons and time at that moment. Granted, I was laughing my ass off as I was saying it.

If I'd had the crayons, it would have been a deeper, more natural, more tactile gut understanding of how the vibrations of colors are integrated into every fractal, and therefore into everything. It is an over-lapping inter-lapping relationship which, I am sure, goes much deeper in the moment. Nobody thought crayons necessary. I think they should be a require-ment. Any four- or five-year-old understands it if you take the time to watch and listen to them closely, have them explain to you what are they are doing, and ask the right questions. Of course, all of this must happen on a day when you are not driven up the wall with an overload of necessary tasks barreling down on you.

I no longer draw fractals, but for a time, later in life, I could perfectly and harmoniously add them to any drawing or sketch whenever I had the time to return to tutoring for math. Improving an attempted piece of art would require time and deep concentration in order to be enjoyed. Fractals were fun. My teacher, who by then was younger than I was, said I reminded her of her older sister. I thought, *Wait, how old am I?* For me, there is no doubt that it's best to return to school when one is older. It is a blast. More of a blast than being young and thinking that just partying is enough to satisfy life.

Wait, aren't adult coloring books all the rage lately? Mandalas are fractals, a repeated pattern that can be quite intricate. Coloring books are an active medita-tion that unties and un-bottles music. Do you find yourself humming, after a while, when coloring? It kind of comes naturally, I think. They are quite beautiful, too. Come to think of it, I bought one once. My girlfriend was having a really hard time with her daughter, so I bought her a coloring book of curse words. You had to look into the patterns to see them. My bad.

When junior year started. I was lonelier than ever, with no friends I could hang out with after school. Rita became pregnant, and gave birth to a little boy, Jackie. That was it—my dad couldn't have been happier. Finally, a son in the family. Of course, it was Rita, *his* Rita, who fulfilled his hopes and dreams.

Time was passing, and little Jackie wasn't doing the things little babies start doing. One eye started crossing inward, and things were really not looking good at all. In our family, the bottom started to fracture even further. It was breaking apart and falling away with every passing day. For Jackie, there was no improvement, and things started getting worse. There was no end to the grief my father was experiencing. Jackie wasn't just autistic: he had layers of developmental trouble. By the time he was diagnosed, the doctor told Rita and Jack not to have any more children, because they didn't know what was causing it, and there was no guarantee it wouldn't happen again. Rita was already pregnant again. Abortion was out of the question; Rita didn't have the constitution to harm anything, especially a child, in any way, shape, or form. Ever. Paul, her second child, was born autistic, but not as severely. Rita had the constitution to rise to the occasion and battle uphill to get her children what they needed, even if she had to carve it out of life itself, at the cost of her own.

Unfortunately, that was the cost Rita paid to make sure her children got what they needed to reach their full potential. Today, Jack is no different, but he is alive. Her strength and ability to love with that kind of devotion opened my eyes to the depth of love required not only of my sister and brother-in-law, but also of other parents. I didn't know it was possible for that kind of love to even exist. I knew that when a child was born sick, or required a lot of attention, men usually cut out and divorce their families. Not Jack. Not Rita and Jack. Their bond got stronger and more beautiful for their endurance. The only way I could describe it is like a cable in an Irish fisherman's sweater. It was full of braids, but the interwoven, difficult things were made into something stronger that weathered life's storms beautifully. It was agony to watch their work and suffering.

My brain couldn't wrap itself around it. I didn't have a hundredth of that unconditional love. Rita told me if it were my children, I would find the strength. I have a brilliant, healthy, handsome son of unlimited talent, and I still find it hard loving him sometimes. No—Rita brought me to shame compared to her selfless, kind, patient, indomitable love. She worked, making sure her children had things like dance classes—everything that would bring them out before it was even heard of at the time. Back then, hiding children who were autistic was acceptable. You kept these children out of sight. Rita and Jack worked in full light. They lived and breathed for their children.

I can't say the same for my father. All he could ever say was, "Why? Why, Rita?" Not one, but two children could not be conceptualized by him. Here was a man who had once been happy, healthy, and hardworking. Maybe he had a strange sense of humor sometimes, but he loved sports, did what he loved, and had a family that supported him—and that he supported. Dad had what he wanted in a wife, and was especially pleased with his first child. He cared with all his heart about the living and the dead, when others recoiled.

Now, he had no mother, sister, niece, or father around. He was completely broken: physically, mentally, emotionally, and spiritually. My dad was completely powerless. The only thing that kept him alive was anger and crying when he thought no one was looking. My daddy was gone. I didn't know this man. It was like loving a rosebush in winter. All thorns.

He used to laugh and say, "Do you know what makes roses beautiful? A lot of horse shit." But now, no one was laughing. It was all inconceivable, and it stunk.

At the time, taking a music class during junior year was a requirement, like art class. I should have known that music class would be a tricky thing for me, and damage even further something I loved.

CHAPTER 14

When Hell Opens Its Gates Wide

JUNIOR YEAR OF HIGH SCHOOL BEGAN. I had been feeling good about myself as far as sophomore year went, and had adjusted to the school and the neighborhood well. I had kept to myself. Now, I was going on sixteen, and needed friends. My high sensitivity kept me away from input overload: places with loud, pounding music or a lot of activity and light around me. I need a much quieter environment and downtime in order to fully enjoy myself. I couldn't bear what was happening in my family alone anymore. I needed a reprieve with a few friends my own age. I needed to be sixteen and have fun, and, for the first time, be able to freely go over to someone's house and hang out after school.

Dad was talking to me again, and I wasn't a topic of concern. I was left on my own. Dad kept saying to me, "Laura, high school is a great time. It was great being in it. I had the time of my life." After his stroke, he started thinking in terms of himself more, and assumed what he had done would work for me, as it had worked for him. So much so that the more time that passed, the more like him I became. We were so much alike, and he kept thinking about the way he used to be before the stroke.

Now that so much time has passed and I can see the truth from a better perspective, I can see that Dad began, ever so slowly, barely noticeably at first, to live through me. The only thing that made us different was the fact that I was not a guy. He always found that hard to distinguish, because he had taught all of us how to build, fix, and design things as naturally as if we were boys. Even picking up things that felt heavier than myself didn't matter. Dad always spoke to me as an equal. When I needed to get a point across, I would call him Leo, and he would listen at attention to what I was saying. He knew I meant what I was saying, and I knew he appreciated it—but of course as an adult, never as a child. Not many people can call their parents by their first names and have it work. It wasn't a habit. It was a point.

Each of us three girls had better skills in different things, but we had to learn how to do all of it. Rita could hang wallpaper like a champ. I liked playing with the plumb tool with the blue chalk. I could play with that all day long and design things on the wall with it. My hanging wallpaper always came out Cubist. When you looked at it, you might have a seizure and not know it.

For Joanne, fractions and precision—and building or doing anything that required them—were among her greatest skills. She eventually worked in accounting. My dad was excellent with precision and numbers. I could fix things. He had me running wires through the ceiling to put in an intercom in the funeral home from the doorway to the back office on the lower level. I like putting things together, adjusting things to make them work; that was always my job. That intercom system is still working great after forty years. When I visited once and saw how well it was working, I said, "What? That thing is still working?" The guys laughed, and said back, "Yeah, you installed it," which really made me laugh. I wasn't going up into the ceiling space crawling across those beams again—I was doing it right the first time. I made sure of it. Beams are hard on the knees. The day I was up there, Cappy, the electrician who had wired the place with Dad, came by for a visit. It was the kind of day I wanted to experience at six: working with them. They were talking about women when I heard Dad say, "Ugh, Cap, Laura's up in the ceiling." Cappy said, "Oh, I'm sorry." They were really into their conversation. They didn't hear me laugh at "too much information." Dad forgot I was there; I was quiet, and just kept working. Waiting to continue.

As soon as I could hold a paintbrush and knew what it was used for, it became my job to paint the radiators. I moved on to windowsills and more. I am still great at using a single-edged razorblade. I learned this by scraping dry paint off windows. I loved using them, and still do. I love tools as sharp as razors, except when I got my first scalpel. I used it on flesh once; I prefer window panes.

The stroke had made Dad powerless. Kind of like when a woman does not have a life of her own and lives her life through her children. She feels if she is not involved to an unhealthy extant in her adult children's lives, she has no value of her own. I can see that now—how painful it must have been for him. When it becomes a matter of who the breadwinner is in the family, that is blurring the lines of gender, and in an old-school Italian family, that usually didn't go over too well. Dad had a very tender side to him, and apparently, he had to pay a price for it. It didn't fit into the way things were supposed to go at the time.

Looking back, I think it started when he couldn't get out of his own way. He was functioning better, but that was not saying much. He still couldn't work, and his friends were still keeping the business open and basically running it for him. He'd gotten his speech back, but still didn't have the strength to drag his body around. He had gotten out of the wheelchair, but it was still in the bedroom, and he spent most of his time in bed.

Mom was stressed to the teeth, and though she cared deeply, there was no backup plan for sharing the burden of raising an adolescent, certainly not when her grandchildren required so much attention. She told me later on, "Laura, I always knew you would land on your feet, so I threw you to the street." She didn't throw me out of the house, but she did leave me to fend for myself. She said, "At that time, I couldn't do anything more. I am sorry. I had my hands full." I understand now. There is only so much one human being can do, and moms always get the blame. I can see now that it killed her to have to do it. She would have preferred to raise a girly girl under her watchful eye. Back then, I thought she liked me, but didn't love me.

That was my introduction and education to being a full-fledged Brooklynite. Landing on my feet. I was on my way. In Brooklyn, it's called Brooklyn street-smarts. You have to navigate streets that are as different as night and day, and maybe a neighborhood a mile long before they change again.

I was getting pretty, but with boobs and what my mom called a "heart-shaped ass," I was starting to become aware of sex—its drive and importance in life. Intimacy was more of what I would have preferred. When you are young, sex, trust, and intimacy are still being determined. The order in which they arrive—especially, sometimes, for a girl—determines the amount of pain one needs to learn through. I was at a disadvantage. I was pretty, left on my own, and still immature and hurting. Perfect prey.

I made a friend. She was in one of my classes, and we started to spent a lot of time together, talking and laughing like girls our age. She lived closer to the school than I did, and going to her house was just easier. Her grandma lived in the downstairs apartment in their two-family home. I liked her grandmother a lot. She was nice to hang out with after school, too. My friend and I had mutual friends, and I knew I was liked and even accepted, just for being myself. It was a good feeling. I spent as much time away from home as I could. Homework was no longer a priority. If I passed, I was happy. If I liked a particular subject, I did well. I didn't really care how happy or mad that made my parents, or if they were disappointed in me or not. It only really mattered if I was happy with myself, really. It was never an issue with Mom. She only cared when I made her aware of any real trouble I was in, and that was determined by how well I had landed on my feet.

Then my friend began having an affair with a married teacher, Bert. I watched in horror as this so-called love affair proceeded. He was a popular teacher, and charismatic. I was friends with her; and she was friends with him, you could say. She thoroughly enjoyed the relationship. They played lover games in front of his wife. She would tell me all about it. She would say things like, "We have a particular word we say that means *I love you*. We say it in front of his wife. She doesn't know what we are saying. It is just so funny." One time, she said, "We are going to a concert together, and we have signals between us." And later on, "We were so happy we didn't get caught."

I would go over to his house, too. He always had kids at his house, and students as friends. I remember there was one kid who was dealing pot. He would go to this particular teacher's house, weigh the pot on a balance scale on his table, bag it, and sell it. He would give or sell some to this teacher. Bert enjoyed getting stoned. One day, he said, "I started taking karate classes with a guy my wife works with. He has a black belt and a dojo." I just thought that was great, and I wanted to take lessons, too. It was all the rage at the time, with the Bruce Lee movies everywhere.

I didn't just see it as fun. I was serious. I liked yoga, and this involved the same principle of meditation. The fact that it could really hurt or maybe even kill someone was of great benefit to me, too. I was living in New York, after all. One could never tell when it would be needed. I thought of it as really good street-smarts. I could protect myself, should I ever have the need to. I learned about my energy body, or *chi*, and how to harness it while experiencing this source of power in me.

Bert told me if my parents would allow it, he would take me with him to the classes and drive me home. I asked my mother, and she flat-out refused. I asked my dad, and he said, "Sure, go ahead, I'll pay for them." I loved my dad. He knew I loved and needed to do things that let my energy loose, that allowed me to focus it and build strength. We both loved the feel of it. He had boxed in the navy, so he knew what a cool thing it would be.

Not my mom. She totally didn't get it. She was afraid. "Leo, girls don't do that, and they may take advantage of her. Leo, listen to me. Girls don't do kara-te," I heard her telling my father as they discussed the matter in their bedroom. My mom was a very smart woman—not about learning karate, but about avoiding being taken advantage of.

Earlier, somewhere along the line, I had been offered a job modeling, and my mom had slapped that guy down so fast it made my head spin. I got angry, because it *was* a job. She saw it as an opportunity to be molested. I blamed her for not loving me. This time, of course, I wouldn't listen to her, or give her the chance to stop me. I only wanted to do what *I* wanted to do. Dad told my mom, "Don't worry, Laura will be fine. I think it's important that she do it." I thought I would be fine, too. After all, this teacher was married. His wife was pregnant by this time, and he had my friend for sex on the side. He was getting enough. I was safe. I just hadn't mentioned that part to my dad. Mom lost the argument.

Dad gave me money, and paid for the lessons and for the *gi*, or uniform. I took Shotokan karate. I was doing well. I loved it. I practiced it a lot, and concentrated hard. I learned how to fall without hurting myself, and even got good enough at it to be in a demonstration. I advanced from a white to a yellow belt, and was looking forward to getting a green belt. I was really enjoying myself, and beginning to feel the *chi* moving in me.

Then, one night as we were driving home, Bert lit a joint. He nudged me, with the joint in his fingers, to try it. "It's good," he said. "Go ahead." I figured I might as well give up and smoke it. My life wasn't my dream life, so I might as well go to hell. I was having some fun, and was lost already. This wasn't the kind of friend I really wanted—a stoned, married man having an affair with his young student. The people I did want as friends worked, and had no time to hang out after school. So I smoked it. I really got stoned, but it made me sick. When we arrived in front of my house, I opened the car door and threw up. I got out, and was just standing there in the street leaning on the vehicle, dizzy. Instead of making sure I got into my house alright, he said,

"Okay," with a look that said *you're all right, right?* I just nodded my head, because I knew he was going to take off like a rat. He shut the door, said, "Bye," and took off really fast. A little too fast for me. It proved he had no spine. At the time, teachers held real power. I had felt threatened by the possibility of him telling my parents, not realizing he couldn't face them himself. That was when I realized what a coward he was. I got into the house safely, but I felt lost and alone anyway. I felt betrayed. Big surprise. I hated school. I wanted out.

I didn't want to hang out with Bert anymore, but I wanted to keep up with karate. His friend wanted to have sex with me, but I wouldn't. The guy was skeevy. They said I must be a lesbian. He must have told my friend that I smoked pot with him, because when she and my other friends got together again, my friend Shirley pulled some joints out and said to me, "We aren't sure if you smoke or not." I looked at my friends around me, looking back and wondering how "cool" I was. I'd given up, and started to smoke at around thirteen. I thought I might as well add more smoke to the clouds already around me. It was easier to avoid being seen in a thicker cloud. Maybe it would help. I smoked the joint.

For my sixteenth birthday, I invited the same three friends over. I had sectioned off the area where my grandmother used to keep her sewing machine, and made a space of my own. I got some chairs, put a rug down, and added a table with a curtain on it. We could hang out there. Nobody was living in the basement at the time. It hadn't been redone yet, so it was cold and damp, but I made it more comfortable. I got into the habit of going in there when I was in a mood and wanted to be alone.

A few days earlier, I had attended another class-mate's sixteenth birthday party. Inez was her name. She was really tall, with long brown hair, and beautiful inside and out. She had a nose job that year, but I liked her just the way she was. Girls weren't accepted as themselves, though. We had to measure up to some kind of desirable picture of what was sexy. We were not okay unless we were sexualized into something that wasn't us. I had never considered something like a nose job a common thing to do, or no big deal. I was learning fast. She was a very nice person.

Her father and mother threw a big party for her in a hall. There were a lot of people there, but I didn't know anyone but Inez. Her family was so nice, and everyone there was so happy. The food was really good. I ate things I had never tasted before, and thoroughly enjoyed myself.

Later, Inez came to school with a box, knowing it was my birthday. She said, "Laura, I thought you might like this." It was a beautiful poncho that could even be worn as a skirt. And that was how I wore it. It was soft, and a deep brown, with a white Southwestern pattern on it. I was so touched and surprised. It was the only sweet sixteen birthday gift I received that made me feel I had any semblance of a genuine life without some kind of pain attached. She had thought of me. That was what kept me going. Maybe there was a chance to have the kind of life I wanted, and honest friends who didn't occupy the shadows.

I was so heartbroken that my parents hadn't thrown me a sweet sixteen party. Now I know they didn't have the money to throw me a party like that. Deep down, I knew that with my dad's stroke and paralysis, he wouldn't be throwing a party anytime soon. I had bought a bottle of Cold Duck wine to celebrate with my friends. It was all I could afford. My mother said she would make pizza. It wasn't my idea of a real celebration.

I had been so looking forward to something special just for me. Two of my friends couldn't make it, or forgot which day it was, or something happened...I don't remember. My "close friend" Shirley just didn't show up, and apparently didn't even care that she hadn't. I wanted privacy from my family, but not so much privacy that none of my friends showed up. So much for picking good friends my own age. I was lousy at it. I drank the whole bottle of wine by myself, and had my head in the toilet for longer than I wanted.

This guy my cousin Janet knew called me, and kept calling while I was barfing. I got disgusted and answered the phone, and he said he wanted to go out with me. I said I didn't think so; I wasn't feeling well, and didn't want to go anywhere. He kept insisting, and wouldn't quit. Just to shut him up and get on with my barfing, I said I would. He picked me up soon after, and pulled up in front of the house in a big black Cadillac. I said to myself, *Oh, no this guy is in the Mafia. Why did I say yes?* I opened the door, and he was about 350 pounds. I thought to myself, *Nothing is going right in my life, this doesn't look like sixteen to me. This is turning out to be a nightmare!!!!* But he was very nice. He took me to Yonkers Raceway, to the horse races. It was the first time I had ever been there. I loved horses, and had a good time. I was not going to kiss him good night, though, and I still wasn't sure if he was "connected" or not. No way did I want to date a Mafia guy. He might not have been, but I wasn't taking any chances.

I gave up on having a boyfriend even close to my age. Guys I liked and showed interest in told me, "You don't want to go out with me. I am not good enough for you." That happened twice. I felt like crap about myself; these guys were good enough to be honest with me, and thought I was too good a person. I couldn't win. Apparently, the good guys wanted no part of me, or I was just unaware that they were flirting with me. I wasn't looking for a boyfriend. Friends were just good enough, and the friends I had were really distant, except for Jacob. He loved me for who I was. He saw through me. He knew I was a benign person, and knew more about pain than the average. He knew about family pain. He bought a jean jacket and asked me if I would embroider it. I used to fix the holes in my jeans with little things I embroidered on them. So I embroidered a nature scene on the back of it. He appreciated it. He loved it. He was marrying Hanna, his girlfriend. They eventually moved out to California together.

With few reprieves that allowed me space to breathe, I experienced crushing lows. Not only did I do poorly in class, but there was a race riot junior year, and it started with me, as far as I knew. I never ate in the lunch room, but there was a girl in the neighborhood whose grandparents moved into the neighborhood when my grandparents did, just two blocks apart. My mom and her mom had fought over the same guys when they were young. Gina and I went to high school together, and as it turned out, her nephew and my son ended up going to grammar school together. We decided one day that we would have lunch together at school rather than leave—it was cheaper. All of a sudden, while we were talking and eating, a Black girl looked at me across her table and said, "I know what you said about my cousin."

"What?" I responded. I looked at Gina and said, "I don't know her or her cousin." I said to the girl, "I don't know your cousin." She got up from her table with four or five other girls, and started coming my way.

Gina and I said together, "Let's get out of here." We got up and went to toss our food out in the bins, which were on the way out. I was going to do exactly what I normally did. I wasn't going to run, but instead walk very fast. Before I knew it, I was surrounded. Not Gina. They didn't include her. It was me. *Oh, shit,* I said to myself. This time, I knew I was dead meat. Regina in St. Joseph's was Italian; we were on equal ground. I hadn't had enough time with this girl for her to not like me.

The girl came up to me really close. She had me beat in every way physically, and I could not take on five girls alone. There had been serious racial tension in the school since African American students had begun to be bussed in. She kept repeating, "I heard what you said about my cousin."

I had never said anything nasty about a Black student. If anyone made a remark, I either ignored them and didn't want any part of them, or said something to them about stopping it. I didn't want to hear it, which usually meant I didn't want people making racist comments to hang out with me. This gave me a clearer picture of what I didn't like about Mill Basin. I didn't have to suffer this type of serious racial divide downtown. I didn't have issues like that with anyone. I was used to living amongst all kinds of people.

This big girl decided she was going to start something physical; it was in her eyes. The school was a tinderbox. She and her friends completely surrounded me, and then she gave me a hard kick in the ass. They all started laughing at me. Gina and I just ran out of school. That, apparently, was the action that lit the match. When Gina and I got back home, we told my mom. Of course, I had to go back the next day. I found out there had been a race riot like nobody's business. A kid had gotten hit in the head with a stick with a nail in it while getting on a bus to get out of there. It was serious. Both Gina and I were so happy to have missed the worst of it. By the next day, with the cops still around, things cooled off—but of course, there was still a low burn.

I just kept on keeping on. Still went to karate, still cut as many classes as I could get away with. Still did well in classes I liked as long as the teachers loved the subjects they taught with a passion. Then, one day in school, I saw Bert, the teacher I was doing karate class with. He said to me, "Before karate class today, do you want to come to my house and practice some?" I was seriously leery, but I didn't think he would really try anything serious, and of course I had already been intimidated by him before with the pot, so I went. My defenses were down because of disappointment in myself after the race riot, and my self-esteem wasn't at its highest.

We arrived at his house. There was no one else there, which made me uncomfortable, but we were just going to practice. We went into his living room and started doing the *katas*. These are exercises that go through all the different defensive and offensive moves. They blend into one another, and if they are practiced often enough, you start learning where your power comes from and how to move to use it most efficiently. It is a dance that can kill someone gracefully, but the whole point is to avoid the use of force. Karate is meant to breed peace, because life demands respect, unless. . . . You know the deal: use the least amount of force to fight, or turn your opponent's own force back on them. It is a powerful discipline: a beautiful thing to practice and to watch, especially when someone does it well.

While we were practicing the exercise, Bert said, "See if you can throw me." This was an agreed-upon practice: using your opponent's energy to throw them down, and practicing falling and going with the energy without getting hurt. Learning that had cost me a lot of black and blues, but I was good at it. Dispersing the energy of hitting the ground was a skill, and it was fun. Learning to throw someone bigger and stronger than myself was a skill that needed more concentration.

All of a sudden, he was all over me. I froze. I didn't know what to do. I was scared that if he told my parents I had seduced him, I would get into trouble, because he could tell them I had been smoking pot. I was over at his house alone, and he was married. What was I doing there alone? Worst of all, my mother would have been proven correct, and then a whole new family conflict would begin. I would have been chained with a chain that went as far as school and back.

Bert was forcing himself on me to have sex, and I wasn't doing anything to stop him. I couldn't—but I also wanted to feel hugged at the same time. He was warm. Well, he was going on half naked, and it wasn't just his top half. *Gis* open easily. Before any penetration occurred, though, he pushed me away, saying, "Three women are too much." Actually, it was probably four. His wife was still pregnant.

Get yourself together. I was a thinner of a shell of a person by the time I got home that night. My soul was leaving me this time, and I began not to care if I was getting meaner. I continued going to karate classes with him, but he didn't take me home. The instructor did. And before long, he had his hands all over my breasts. Now I was getting pissed off. Then the karate teacher told me he wanted me to meet his wife. Before he took me home, he brought me up to his apartment with the excuse of getting something. His wife was stunningly beautiful, as nice as anything, and pregnant. I felt sick.

Bert started going to karate less and less, which was fine by me. One day, though, he showed up, and we were practicing throwing punches. He was standing with his back to the wall at least three feet away, and needed room to step back. I decided I'd had enough of that creep and being taken advantage of and used. In class, I had become clear-headed enough in the moment, and had begun to land on my feet.

This time, I decided that if he wanted to play strong man, let's see how good I could be at it. I threw a passionate, focused punch. I concentrated all my energy, and made it connect with his solar plexus. He flew up against the wall and dropped. He had not been expecting it, and lost his breath. He had decided to connect with me in a too-touchy way. When he eventually got up, he was rubbing his heart area, and said in surprise, "Why did you do that?" I looked, grinned, shrugged my shoulders, and raised an eyebrow, like, *I just felt like it; it seemed a good thing to do at the moment.* I figured if this schmuck couldn't figure it out, he needed to go back to high school.

Bert stopped going to karate after that, and I kept far away from him. I didn't want to go on living. There was an emotional violence no matter where I turned, and even inside of me. I was a big disappointment to myself; this wasn't how it was supposed to go. My self-esteem knew no bottom, it seemed. It wasn't all bad, though. I was learning to be streetwise. That was how junior year ended . . . with me in hell.

CHAPTER 15

And Life Goes On

I FLUNKED GEOMETRY AGAIN. Back to summer school. This time, Joanne was going to Queens College and taking classes during the summer, as well. She had a car, and asked me if I wanted to audit an Art History class she was taking. *Art?* The world in which I had been living just blew away, like a wish on a dandelion in a summer breeze. I was flunking geometry in summer school again. I still went every day, though; I wasn't giving up! But I went to the first art class with Joanne, and we asked the teacher if it was okay if I sat in on his class. When he saw how much I wanted to, he said with a big smile, "Yes, you can stay."

The Art History teacher, Ted, was a great instructor and a really nice guy. He was tall, and probably in his mid-thirties. He was very fit, and shaved his head bald, but he looked great that way. He was very kind, and he was also very hot. I learned about the details of classic paintings, the different types of Roman and Greek columns and architecture. A world of beauty and history opened up for me. I hadn't felt that happy to be alive since I couldn't remember when. He was such a good teacher, pointing out details you would never see in a painting unless you were shown, like reflections in a small mirror in a painting that were one-inch duplicates of what you were looking at. I was completely absorbed, and in awe.

About twenty-five years later, Rita invited me on an outing with her Art History class to the Cloisters. I even found a frog in the tapestry of the story of the unicorn. The tapestry was hundreds of years old. It was the last thing Rita and I did together that was special before she died. I was the only one in the entire class to find the hidden frog. Rita said to me, "You are amazing." I just smiled, thought of Ted, and agreed with her. It was a sunny day. The funny thing was, I'd never taken an Art History class of my own in my entire life. I recommend having good sisters.

The frog, I learned, represented marriage. Maybe the people who made the tapestry and knew the story of the unicorn also knew about marrying a frog. They never knew if kissing one would turn him into a prince or not, I guess. The unicorn was representative of Christ. The tip of his horn purified anything it touched, especially water. Only a virgin could capture a unicorn.

No frogs wanted to be involved with unicorns, I guess.

In the Bronx, not too far from the Cloisters, there is tile art on the walls of one of the subway stations depicting a unicorn picking up litter with the tip of his horn rather than a litter stick. If you wonder why I am a bit nuts, come to New York and stay a few years.

In any case, it was Joanne's teacher who honed my eye. I was doing really well in the course, and Ted asked me out one time after class. He told me I could call him by his first name. I had always wanted to let him know how great the class was. I was thrilled he'd asked me out, and was so comfortable with him. We walked over the Brooklyn Bridge together. Passing one of the cables, he said, "Want to see something I can do?"

"Sure," I replied. He grabbed onto one the cables with both hands and brought himself up sideways, perpendicular to the cables. He was at a right angle to the cables of the bridge!!! I could see him shaking from the effort, but he did it with his own strength. Then he brought himself down again, and we both started laughing because it was so cool. It was great. Now that was my idea of geometry!!!

We walked into Chinatown, and Ted bought me something to eat. Then he took me home. This was a highlight in my life God provided to help me see that very good people did exist, who asked for nothing and just enjoyed being. Stars by which to navigate in a dark sky.

I will never forget him; that was when I learned what intimacy was. It is someone who sees you, and you them, and the thoughts and feelings are completely honest. Sex is not needed to prove manhood.

Genuine kindness and genuine interest bring so much more. It is life-giving.

After that, Joanne and I took the final exam. She was already pissed off because Ted had taken such an interest in me, and was so good looking. In class, I was asking questions all over the place, and answering questions as often as Ted called on me. I didn't always get them right, but I was learning. I was just another student in that class, and it was a college course. In the end, Joanne told me, "You are lucky. If you had gotten a better grade than me, I would have killed you." I legitimately earned the grade I was given. I never studied for any test we took, but she did. Our grades were very close. I think I got a B+, and Joanne got an A. I could enjoy it without the worry of improving my grade index. I just went to class, and had a blast. It kept me breathing.

The summer ended, and I found myself back at South Shore. It didn't take long for me to be sucked down in the mire of despair, and hating myself for what I had been involved with in the previous spring. I got my class schedule: I had been given geometry again for the first half of senior year. I stopped going to school. It was a daily reminder of what a failure I was.

One time, when I did show up, I heard that there was going to be a fight at a certain time. I came home early, and happened to mention it to my mom. I was called back to school and into the principal's office. From there, I was brought into a room with the people who were going to fight and with a bunch of other people. *Oh, damn* was my first thought. *Here is where*

I get beaten up for sure. I denied saying anything about it. It turned into a discussion, and everyone left having made peace. It was good. Later on, my mom told me, "You know, Laura, I called the school and told them what you told me about the fight." I was quiet, but thought to myself. *That, Ma, is not a big surprise. This time, you're in luck. If I had gotten beaten up because it was me who opened my mouth about it, I don't know what I would have done.*

Things were not getting better. Cigarettes, pot, booze . . . nothing was self-medicating me enough against being so alone and just imploding. Mom saw there was something seriously wrong, but I wasn't saying anything. She took me to an endocrinologist, thinking maybe something was wrong with my thyroid. He was a good doctor, and he saw right through me. He said that the way I was feeling was what some women experience before they get married. He was right, but I still wasn't telling my mother anything, and neither did he. It felt good knowing he knew what got me down so much. He gave me these pills that made it feel like I was on speed. I stopped after taking them twice. I hated the way they made me feel; it was even worse. I was pretty hopeless, at this point, of being cared for at all by anyone. It didn't matter anymore. I didn't want to live. Moments of kindness weren't enough to keep me wanting to go on. The thought of suicide was not out of the picture.

I tried hiding that I wasn't going to school from my parents. One night, as I was taking a shower, the phone rang, and I didn't hear it. My mom knocked on the bathroom door and said, "Mr. Nissen is on the phone; he wants to talk to you." I turned chalk white. Mr. Nissen was the dean, and he didn't joke around. I was in trouble, and I knew it. I said, "I'll be out in a minute." I was out of that shower in a flash, and grabbed the phone from my mother's hand before he had the chance to say anything to her.

I answered the phone. "Hi, Mr. Nissen." I knew who he was, but he didn't know me right off the bat.

He said, "You know you haven't been going to school, and it looks like you are not going to graduate."

"Yeah, I know."

He thought a second, and said, "Wait, I know you. I know who your friends are." And he gave a laugh as if to say, *Yeah, friends.* Then he thought and said, "You're smart." I didn't say anything. "I don't care why you haven't been to school," he continued. "Just get your ass in here tomorrow, and meet me in my office." Then he hung up. I thought, *Thank God he didn't tell my mom anything.*

I showed up at school the next morning. On my way to Mr. Nissen's office, I saw him: this big bruiser of a guy walking toward me with a bunch of papers in his hand. I didn't know what I was more scared of, him or flunking out. As he came up to me, he said, "Listen, you failed a lot of classes last semester." By this time, it was the last semester of my senior year. He said, "I got you doubled on the classes you have to make up. That means Chemistry 1 and Chemistry 2, and History 3 and 4. You will have gym in the morning and after lunchtime. Forget Geometry—I convinced them to give you a Logic class." He just kept going until I had eight full periods. He said, "You are going to graduate. Do you hear me?"

I took in a deep breath, let it go, and said, "Yes, Mr. Nissen."

"Here is your schedule. Now go." And so I did. I had Regents Exams that year in Chemistry, History, and God know what else. It was those two I was worried about. Plus, I had the SATs at the end of the school year.

With one of my history teachers, it would have been better if I had shot myself back in the 18th century. That guy was so slow, and droned on in a boring way. If I passed the class, it would be a miracle.

As it turned out, Mr. Nissen taught Chemistry. He was actually an excellent teacher. A natural, as any good teacher who loved the subject he taught. He didn't fool around. He worked hard to help you learn, but you had to work for your grade. I was dead meat. Chemistry crossed my eyes only a little less than geometry. I managed to do well in all my classes, but I knew the history and chemistry Regents Exams would either allow me to graduate on time or force me to remain behind for make-up classes.

I figured out that I actually liked history. I could force myself to do the homework despite the teacher and droning on. But Chemistry 1 and 2 at the same time? My brain needed an ironing-out. I had to get it all straight, and definitely needed tutoring. It was going to take a miracle. One day, in class, I asked Mr. Nissen if he could help me understand it; I was in over my head. "Sure, of course, he said. "Meet me in the Chem lab." I don't remember if it was during lunch or after class, I couldn't say—but I did meet him. We sat at the Chemistry table, and he explained it to me so simply that after a little bit of time, it actually made sense! I was so happy.

It didn't take long before I was in over my head again, so I asked, "Show me how this worked?" I was getting into serious trouble with it, and finals and the Regents were coming up. I was passing everything so far, but Chemistry still needed some serious explaining. I was barely getting by.

"Okay," he said. We met again in the lab, but this time, he didn't spend as much time explaining it. He told me, "Listen, I grade the Regents. I can always change your grade." Then he started like moaning and groaning, and he kissed me. I went limp. I couldn't believe this was happening again! I needed help in Chemistry, not chemistry between people. He was married, and also had children; I think his wife had given birth that year, too.

I was getting so angry at the cost of wanting to learn, but then having to learn to protect myself just to get through it. I felt like I was just being passed around. Finally, one day when I asked for help, we went into the lab and he started kissing me again. I said to him, "I came in here for help, and to understand this stuff." "Yes, you are the best student I ever had." My response was, "You touch me one more time, and I promise I will throw acid on your face." The funny thing was, I meant it. I was almost looking forward to it. I had been destroyed by these adult men who were charged with keeping me safe. Seeing that my life was successful according to how well they did as teachers was what they were getting paid for. My grades and my life were in these guys' hands. He looked at me and said, "I just got a new Mercedes I am going to name after you: 'The Bitch.'" I thought to myself, *You do that, because I am going to bide my time and become such a good bitch, your head is going to spin.*

School was ending. I took my finals and passed the classes I didn't like by the skin of my teeth, but I came out close to an eighty-five average. I had passed the History Regents, not with a great grade, but I didn't care. Now it came to Chemistry. I went to the board where the results were posted, and I think I got a sixty-seven. I had passed it—by two points, mind you, but I had passed it. I wondered if Mr. Nissen had changed my grade. I didn't see him around. Finally, I saw him, and he came up to me, smiling and happy. He said, "Laura, you passed it! You passed it on your own! I had to go to court with some kid who was in trouble. I didn't do anything to it! You did it on your own!" I thought, *Thank God. Now I can get the fuck outta here!!!* I started getting cramps, and my mom took me to the doctor. He found a cyst on my ovary that had to be removed. The surgery was scheduled for the day after graduation.

I did well on the SATs. My gym teacher told me one day when we were passing in the hall, "Laura, you won a scholarship from the SATs! Congratulations!" I said, "How nice," and never even bothered to do anything about it. My guidance counselor, after interviewing me about where my future was headed, sat back in his chair and said, "So, you will be a jack of all trades and a master of none."

I said, "Yeah, that's it, thank you," and walked out of his office. I was so happy to have done well, so happy to have graduated, and so jaded I didn't care anymore.

CHAPTER 16

Off to Work We Go

I GRADUATED INTO BECOMING AN ADULT. I was fine after the operation, and spent the time on the beach and smoked pot all summer. I had gotten my driver's license, but never wanted a car and never bought a car. I did everything possible to get as far from my past as possible. My determination was on track. Now that I was out of high school, I went back to school, and loved every minute of it.

Brooklyn provided college courses in local high schools, so I registered, and decided my major would be English, my minor Psychology. Even in the silliness of youth, I aced the classes. Silliness? Maybe that wasn't a good word. Defiance is a better one.

My cousin needed to go to the three-hour class in driving instructions in order to get her license. I took her to it. It was near where I used to go to summer school. This wasn't an issue. My mom only drove her car in the neighborhood for food shopping, etc., so I used it when I needed it. Janet and I were smoking so much pot, it looked like there was a smoke machine going inside the car. We were having a good time even though there was no parking, and it was getting late.

I was determined to get her to class on time. After all, she had to learn how to drive responsibly. There was a cop car parked in front of us and I had to get around it, but with the traffic, it was taking too much time, so I started honking at the cop car like I would any other car to *Get out of the way already!* All of a sudden, the cop came out of his car and started walking toward us. "Uh-oh," I said.

Janet went through her purse in a flash, and started spraying perfume like crazy. The cop came to my window, and when I rolled it down, a cloud of smoke came out of the window so thick I think the cop got an instant high. I said, "Officer, I am taking my cousin to a driving class and I am late. Can you move, please?" He looked into the car, looked at both of us stoned as the Eastern Wall, then said, "Okay." He got into his car and pulled away. Janet and I gave each other a look that said, *Did I just do that? Did he just do that?* I found a parking space, and we ran into the class a little late, but nearly died laughing. Brooklyn savvy had been etched into me since high school. That was the first time I truly realized it, though.

I met my real first boyfriend in one of those college classes. Tony was the only Italian guy I ever dated. He was a fireman, and had a Jaguar sports car. Talk about lucking out. He used to take me to one of the big local empty parking lots and let me drive it any way I wanted to, except if I went too fast. He was a nice guy, but he wasn't taking any chances with me and that Jag. He spent just about every penny he made on that car and its upkeep. It was silver, and it was just something else.

I was still hanging out with some of my high school friends, and got toasted one night. I was still drinking at the time, but alcohol wasn't my drug of choice; pot was. I remembered the bottle of Cold Duck and wasn't going to throw up again, but nevertheless, I came home hanging on the bannister while attempting to get up the stairs. My intention was to slip into my bedroom quietly, unnoticed. I was practically cross-eyed.

My mom was in the kitchen, and I said to myself, *Oh, boy, I am going to get busted.* Instead, she stopped me and said, "Laura." I turned around and faced her dead on. The way she had said my name was way too serious, but she'd said it in a whisper. I knew something was up.

"What is it, Ma?" I said.

She looked at me nervously, and replied, "Your father is going to lose the funeral home, and he's saving up sleeping pills and won't let me touch them." I began to realize what she was saying, even though I was still worried about being busted. I looked at her and realized I was not busted, but shattered. I knew what that meant. If he was going to kill himself, NOBODY was going to stop him.

Then, with pleading eyes, she said, "Laura, Al suggested that if you went into the business with Dad, it would make him want to live, and he wouldn't kill himself." Al was one of their friends.

I was still out of it, but sobering up fast. I needed to think about this. It was the last thing I wanted to do. Since Bobby died, I had sworn I would never have anything to do with it, ever. It was not expected of any of us three girls to go into it. I was going to be an English teacher and do what I loved, especially women's literature. I had registered at the college by this time, and had a full schedule. This was not happening. I thought, *Okay, I am just going to go into my room and sober up completely, to be able to digest this.*

As I passed his door, my father called me in. "Laura? Come here." *Oh, no,* I thought to myself. He sounded bright-eyed and bushy-tailed. I knew I was no match for him. He was sober; I could barely stand up, for two reasons now. Dad was sitting up in bed, with life in his eyes I hadn't seen in ages. My heart melted and broke at the same time. Then he said, "How would you like to come into the business with me?" I thought, *I know I am not thinking clearly. But . . . I could never live my life as a secretary.* I had never discussed my plans for the future with my parents. If I had a license in my back pocket, I could always make a good living, should something ever happen to my husband when I got married . . . whenever that might be. The thing was, I never saw myself owning the family business. Had I visualized that, I probably would have killed myself with his pills.

I looked at Dad. He was filled with enthusiasm. What could I do? I stuffed my life so deep inside of me, I felt like it died. I would never have what made *me* enthusiastic again. I was over and done with.

Oy, I thought. *Here goes.* "Okay," I said. That was it. I went to my room, as frozen and cold as a corpse myself. I heard my mom go into their room, heard my parents talking like there was life in the house again.

Before I knew it, Dad had laid out all the requirements before me on the kitchen table. He told me over coffee, "You would have to have at least thirty college credits; the following year you will register in March at McAllister's (funeral directing school). That's when their spring semester starts. You will have to do a year's residency before you're licensed. You won't be embalming; I have someone to do that. His name is Seb. And you will start to take over Goldie's job, and start dressing and putting the makeup on the corpses." I didn't know morgue duty in Bellevue Morgue was waiting for me. I was eighteen.

I had to take many required courses in college, and I took as many English and Psych classes as I could squeeze in and get away with. I had to think of a better reason why I would want to do this. Not being a secretary was not going to cut it. Since I'd need a miracle to survive this, I went and found my ol' buddy God again. I remembered that caring for the dead was a Corporal Work of Mercy. I said okay to God, and because of that, this was going to be more of a spiritual business for me. I could live with myself now that my joy was over; I had a purpose. I liked science a lot, and knew I could find my buddy to talk to me through it. That perspective was what got me as enthusiastic as I could get. This was now my chosen profession.

College went quickly. I had to drive about twenty minutes to get there. I made a friend, and I took what I liked. I just shut down at the thought of funeral school, but I had to laugh about where life was leading me. It never failed: as soon as I said I would never do something, I found it was the next thing I'd be doing. It was funny, so I threw my hands up, and thought, *Oh well, might as well go along for the ride*, like when I had almost drowned as a child. An adventure is an adventure.

Right before I went off to McAllister's, my grandmother, now eighty, had a cancerous kidney removed. She was as tough as nails, and we knew this was going to faze her about as much as cutting a chicken's head off. She was scared, no question about it. Grandma didn't trust hospitals. She always said, "That's where you go to die." But as soon as she was out of the ICU, she had the nurses brushing her hair a number of times a day. Janet went and did her nails. She got a massage every day from the nurses, and somewhere along the line, her doctor showed her some exercises. She did them religiously.

CHAPTER 17

Learning All about Death,
Big Apple Style: Oy Vey

I TOOK A DEEP BREATH, and bought clothes suitable for school in Manhattan on Park Avenue South, near Union Square—so named because it is a historic intersection where Broadway and Fourth Avenue intersect. A few blocks away is Pete's Tavern, where it is said that O. Henry wrote "The Gift of the Magi," one of my favorite stories as a child. The building was built in 1829, and in 1926, it became Pete's Tavern. It is in the Gramercy Park Area District. Posh is a pretty good way to describe it. Pete's Tavern is still a warm, welcoming place to eat and drink.

Dad wasn't cutting me any money that even came close to posh clothing. I was going to school—functional for the purpose was good enough. Oh well, you can only try, right? I bought nice dresses, black pants, and sweaters at a local store that had good, up-to-date clothing. I bought a dress with wide black-and-white diagonal stripes. I liked it a lot, and chose to wear it the first day of school. I didn't know what to expect of this place called American Academy McAllister Institute of Funeral Service, Inc. My class was the one that celebrated McAllister's Golden Anniversary (1926 to 1976). Okay, it was a privilege, and it was the first time I felt institutionalized. It was nuts there. I was taking the bus and train to get to school again. Reminders of good old St. Joe's. The rush-hour traffic was exhausting.

When I walked into the building, it was old and dark, with a decrepit elevator that reminded me I was going to a school geared toward funerals. I took my life in my hands every time I stepped into it. I said a prayer, "*Lord, please let me live,*" in my soul as it rattled and shook up and down the floors.

The only thing that gave the school life was the fact that in the corner, when you first walked into the building, there was a one-man candy and newspaper stand. The older guy who ran it was a sweetheart. He just loved what he did, and was happy to provide local and world news, plus something sweet to remind you that life wasn't always a deadly experience. Yet.

Coming out of that elevator for the first time with my life was a sign that I could survive this. All classes were held on one floor, with the office nearest the entrance. There were four women administrators who were rarely out of the office, one female lab assistant, ten female students, sixteen male teachers, and forty-seven male students. Out of seventy-eight people on one floor, there were fifteen women to sixty-three men. We tended to get lost, especially since most of us were shorter than the guys.

I walked into my first class, Anatomy, taught by Mr. McAllister himself, and sat down. He came into the classroom looking old as the day is long, and as skinny as the skeleton in the corner. Standing straight with a pile of papers in his arm, he held himself very tall, put his papers down, and greeted us with, "Good morning, gentlemen." He looked right at me as he scanned the class and smiled. My first thought was, *When did I disappear and turn into a gentleman?* Mr. McAllister didn't see women, just addressed us politely when spoken to.

Six of us were from the boroughs of Brooklyn, Staten Island, and Queens. The other four were from Connecticut, Pennsylvania, and South Carolina. The guys covered Connecticut, Long Island, New York City, upstate New York, New Jersey, Maryland, and Pennsylvania. Only one woman was not a member of a funeral home family, and she was wearing the same dress I was. I laughed; she got angry. We became the best of friends.

We had Anatomy, Chemistry, Accounting, Mortuary and Public Health Law, Microbiology, Restorative Art and Cosmetology (learning how to reconstruct a face due to an accident, disease, etc.), Psychology, Funeral Service Principles and Counseling, and, last but not least, Embalming. It was no joke. If you didn't pass one class, or caused a ruckus, you were out on your ear—thrown out. With no refund. We students knew immediately that we were all in this together. It was definitely stressful, and the skeleton in Anatomy class was often found with a cigarette in his mouth.

Jackie, the woman from Connecticut, had a room in the Parkside Residence for Women. It was directly across from Gramercy Park, which was kept locked all the time. The Residence had a key, and it had to be requested, with a strong eye as to who had it. The place was run by the Salvation Army.

After about a month of traveling back and forth to Brooklyn, I was beginning to wear out. This was not fun; it was a to-the-max workload, mentally, emotionally, and physically. Those books weighed a ton. It was as close to a pre-med school as you could get, and with the same pressure to pass. I mean, I loved science, and one (or, at most, two) science classes a year would have given me time to fully appreciate the subject matter. I would have preferred it, but that was not the deal.

A good number of the people at McAllister were embalming already, working behind the scenes and being taught by family members beforehand. I had only experienced and learned the spiritual end of things. I was okay with learning the scientific aspects, but I wasn't going to be embalming unless that assistance was needed. My dad would not allow me near embalming as a child. Things have changed a lot since then. Now, it is required that you take additional credits each year to keep up with health standards, especially with communicable diseases and law—a minimum of six, from what I understand, and maybe more.

I knew a guy who had a little girl as young as I had been when curiosity got the best of me. He brought her into the embalming room and taught her how to perform this particular operation, and she loved it. Who knows if she became a doctor, or went into the medical field if not the funeral business.

Jackie came up to me one day and said, "Hey, Laura, I have a double room in the place. A single one was too small, and didn't have a private bathroom. My parents are wondering if you want to move in with me. It has two beds, dressers, and desks." My ears perked up like a bunny sniffing a field of carrots that had just popped up out of nowhere. She said, "My parents are going to ask your father." That was polite, but there was no way in hell I *wasn't* moving to the city within a block or two of the school in such a neighborhood. There was way too much to explore. The East Village was within walking distance. Washington Square Park in Greenwich Village was THE place to be to offset the drudgery of school.

Jackie's parents were a lot like my parents. She worked as hard as my dad embalming, and had no problem with any part of it. Me? Going to art school would have made me happier. Anatomy was still somewhere in my subconscious.

I asked her, "Why do your parents want me to live with you?"

Her response was, "Well, you are from New York. I'm from far away—Connecticut. They feel that because you know it here, and are not a troublemaker or wild, I'd be safer not being alone here in New York City."

I looked at her, knowing there was no way in hell she wasn't wild. Trouble was her second name.

Within one weekend, I had moved in. The following weekend, I was sitting in Pete's Tavern learning the finer points of drinking so I wouldn't throw up as fast. Jackie's parents owned a liquor store in Connecticut. I was sure she had tasted everything on every shelf. She started me off with something I never had tasted before: a White Russian. It went down so easy, but I knew when I went to stand up that I could go down just as fast.

We had a blast, but I was sticking to White Russians. I loved them so much. We explored every inch of the surrounding neighborhoods within walking distance. She had an older Volvo, but we never drove anywhere in it. Parking was usually nowhere to be found. She just drove it back and forth to Connecticut when she needed to for whatever reason. She would take the train home on weekends, and I went back to Brooklyn to recover from the entire experience of the previous five days. We would leave after school on Friday, and come back Sunday afternoon.

We got the keys and sat in Gramercy Park across the street. On Irving Place, which was around the corner to the right, there was a three-floor building I knew had to be owned by someone with money up the wazoo. All the homes were over the top there. We had it timed when to walk to this particular place every day, just to see if the butler had polished the brass address next to the front door. Every day, it was done. We would take bets on how long it would take him when it rained to get back to polishing it. Only once during that entire year was it done later in the day.

There was also an apparently moneyed gallery to

the left of our building, because famous stars could be seen every now and then walking upstairs to the entrance. The homes on the other side of the Park could make your jaw drop from the money they cost. You could tell from their quality. They made no bones about quietly showing it off, either. So classy. So peaceful.

If you turned the corner to the left, your chances of being run over by traffic a few times wouldn't be noticed. Walk to the right, turn the corner, and you walked into quiet money. Being in school and learning about every cell and cause of death made it funny how equal all of us are, from the homeless on the Bowery to the well-heeled. No one who ended up being autopsied in Bellevue Morgue would know the difference. Bellevue Hospital was a high-standard institution that took care of all the immigrants arriving in New York when the greatest influx came in. They came up with new cures and medications, when needed. In New York today, when you mention Bellevue Hospital, all that comes up in people's minds is the mental ward a.k.a. The Flight Deck, as it is known by many.

As soon as it got warm enough to sit on the stoop of the Residence, we would go and buy the best pizza on the east side of Manhattan and the coldest beer we could get, and just watch life and death pass in front of us, processing it behind our eyes. The area was much more laid back then. You could eat in the local restaurants and feel at home with delicious food. Now, you walk in knowing you are coming out minus an arm and a leg, but with the ability to say that you ate in that restaurant. Its name would change to a different one in a pretty short time. New York City was not a boring place, to say the least. We walked from Park Avenue to First Ave. and down to the East Village. Even Bellevue Morgue was walking distance away.

Jackie was an only child, and her parents had no place to really spend their money except on her. Her grandparents were from Portugal. I loved her grandfather as much as my own, and like mine, her grandmother was as tough as nails. The first time I visited her home in Connecticut, her father had a heart attack. We spent most of the night in the hospital. They apologized to me. I couldn't believe it; I loved them. They gave my mother a plant when they came over for dinner once—a philodendron. It grew for over thirty years in the window, and hundreds of cuttings were made. That family was just home to me.

We were all hanging by a thread at school. Lifelong friendships were made. In Restorative Art class, if you were chewing gum, you were thrown out immediately. The guys were being thrown out just for fun by Mr. Mayer; they would come up with the stupidest of reasons to get thrown out. Everyone knew the teacher was really laid back. He was drunk most of the time. For fun, I never gave him a reason to throw me out. He was itching to—don't ask me why. It was more of a game, but quite honestly, I loved that class. Not only was it working and practicing with clay, it was also learning how to make a head out of clay. I had taken one art class in high school. This was learning how to make it perfectly true to life.

Most of the guys already knew how to do it, or were familiar with it from their own family funeral homes. In my yearbook, Mr. Mayer wrote, "Sorry I never had the chance to throw you out."

I said, "Me, too." I think he knew I wanted to be thrown out of more than just his class. He just made me feel good by saying it. It was so stressful. You could see how many of the teachers were coming in drunk. Students had hangovers, and the rest were smoking pot in the stairways. We passed by mercy's sake alone.

Things were going along as usual. The guys knew which teachers they could make fun of because of the subjects they taught, and rarely called them by their real names. Dr. Pokorny taught Microbiology and Public Health. The guy was brilliant, and just loved microbiology. He drew a mosquito on the chalkboard with all its organs so perfectly that if you had a hangover that day, you were just waiting for that sucker to fly off the board and inject you any second. He hated pigeons with a passion because of the health issues they presented. So the guys in the back of the room would open the windows and make pigeon calls. After a while, they were just ignored, and you just listened to what Dr. Pokorny was teaching. In minutes, you'd be zoned out trying to absorb what he was talking about, because he would go off on tangents. He was a big older man with white hair. That guy was as gentle as you could get.

One time, I walked into his office just to say hello and chat. Before long, the subject we were talking about had changed somehow to his explaining, "When you autopsy a dolphin, this is what you'll find."

I said, "Okay, Dr. Pokorny, gotta go, have a nice day." I walked out, thinking, *What the hell? How did we get on the subject of dissecting dolphins?* He was so passionate about his work that at any moment, I could have pulled up a chair and just sat in front of him with my jaw dropped, listening to how much he knew. The guys called him Popcorn.

If you didn't develop a sense of humor or took yourself too seriously, the school could break you. It never let up. You were held to a professional decorum until you almost broke. Then you could just kick back and get drunk, and start laughing about watching that skeleton find himself in the casket that hung by the doorway of one of the classrooms. He was once found with a joint in his mouth. That was taken down fast, before anyone could get busted. I had to laugh.

Then it turned to summer. New York has hot, humid summers that can exceed a hundred degrees. It was one of those summers. I was smoking pot just to relax, drinking with dinner, and just enjoying myself at night whenever I could. By then, Embalming was one of the classes that had to be taken. It was the one class I was not happy to attend. A group of us were walking to the morgue the first day, and the reality hit me that this was not what I had signed up for in life. I was done; I wanted out. But the fact that his daughter "was going into business with him" brought my dad to life. There was no other female funeral director in the vicinity. I was the only woman in the area, the most important part of Brooklyn. I could have left in a split second, but I couldn't do that to him.

As we got closer and it became clear there was no

turning back, I said to one of the guys, "You got a joint?" They were always available, one way or another; someone always had one. A couple of the women didn't smoke or drink anything. They were the rare ones, but they could not take themselves seriously, and managed to stay cold sober with a great sense of humor. I didn't know how long they had been familiar with the business, but they were willing to do what they needed to do to get out and get back to what they knew and had chosen willingly.

I thought to myself, *I can't go in there; I already have a hangover from last night's drinking, trying to blot out walking into that morgue. I don't need to face that head-on with only one frayed nerve left.* So I lit the joint and I passed it along on the streets of New York to anyone who wanted it. Nobody cared, nor was it anything unusual at that time—unless you walked straight into a cop.

So I smoked some of it, not all, just enough to try to relax. I knew I was going to have to learn how to embalm someone from start to finish and participate in this operation. There was no way they were going to let me slide. *I never signed up for this*, I thought—then remembered, *Uh-oh, I did.* I told myself, *okay, another adventure. You only live once. Why not learn and experience as much as life offers you?* I just had to experience this, whether I liked it or not. We all walked in the front door. I was immediately hit with the smell of human decomposition. I suggest that if you get the chance to avoid that odor for your entire life, take it. That is all I am going to say about it. It is something you could live without knowing. The fact that it was one of those New York summer days didn't make it any easier. It was not air-conditioned in there. We walked in, and were told we had to wait a minute. I passed the guy at the desk as my eyes began to adjust from the sunlight outside.

I looked the place over, and saw crates stacked up from floor to ceiling. Crates of body parts. Some had blood that just dripped down from them. It was obvious what they were. My head cleared as soon as I fully realized what I was looking at. I said to the guy at the desk, "What happened?"

He looked to the crates and said, "Airplane crash." I hadn't heard anything about it. Then I realized there are many things under the sun that are no big deal and not newsworthy due to their frequency in New York. It could have been from somewhere else, and Bellevue had the expertise to identify the pieces and parts. They taught us about airplane crashes and what they do to the human body, and what to expect and recognize in terms of where the person was sitting in the plane. I said to myself, now that I was as clear as a bell, *Okay, I can handle this. I know about this.* They didn't want us hanging out in the doorway, so they told us which room to go to. We all piled in. There were six of us at a time in each room, with one corpse to work on. Our room had a porcelain table with this dead man on it. I looked him over, thinking this was the guy we were going to embalm. Genitals are always covered on the dead out of human respect. This guy was gorgeous! He was built up, and his muscles were all defined from exercise. He might have been in his late twenties or early thirties, handsome as anything with dark brown hair. I couldn't believe anything was wrong with him that would have put him on that table. Then I looked down at his legs to his feet. His feet looked as if they had been put on backwards. Two guys were taking him off the table and moving him onto a gurney. I asked, "What did he die of?" I couldn't think at that point.

One of the guys said, "Suicide." I thought to myself, *This guy is healthy and beautiful. Why would he kill himself?* As I was watching them move him off the table, they started to struggle. When they dropped him, I heard the back of his head squish. The next thing I remember, I started to sway, and someone told the teacher, "Laura's turning green."

This gentle man stood in front of me so I wouldn't absorb any more information about this. He said, "Go outside and get some air." It was with the understanding I was coming back to work. I don't remember going outside past the crates. I had my head down, and my eyes on the floor. I was doing everything I could not to pass out. I knew if I got away from that smell, chances were good I wouldn't barf everywhere. I took my time outside, and made sure my lungs were breathing fresh air, my stomach was where it belonged, and my courage and sense of responsibility had been restored.

I gathered myself together and walked back into the room. This time, there was a Bowery bum who had been frozen for three months on the table. I knew, because I asked. The teacher said to me, "I know your dad, and I know you won't be embalming so just scrub the bodies down." And so I did—every one that we worked on. I wasn't alone; we were all doing different parts. Only Ajax and a brush were getting this guy clean from being on the street for so long.

One day, I was standing in an alcove in the same room when I noticed an extra ripe smell I couldn't move away from. The windows were open, but it seemed thicker than usual in the spot where I was standing. I looked down, and there was a skull in a crate, looking at me with skin stuck all on the sides of the box. I said hi to him and thought, *Floater, East River maybe, murdered, most likely.* I smiled at him, said, "Bye," and walked over to the table to get to work.

Then the teacher said to me, "You know, I will get into trouble and can't pass you unless you pick up at least one artery." We were all given a set of surgical tools. I used a long-nosed clamp to hold roaches so I wouldn't burn myself when I was smoking a joint. I took out my kit, opened it up, took out my scalpel, and went to cut through this guy's skin.

I said a prayer for him before I cut. His skin was as tough as rawhide. I made the cut, found the artery, and lifted it. That was it. I had done it. My requirement was finished.

We were given a tour of the upstairs Forensic Museum. *Oh, yippy*, I thought, *we get to go on a little field trip upstairs.* Everything in it represented some kind of unique death. I remember looking into a jar and there was this guy's throat with a hunk of meat in it so big it had suffocated him. That will be a lesson to you to cut your meat into bite-sized pieces. Then there was one of those gates you can open and close like scissors. There was a guy's shoe stuck in it. Electrocution. "Okay, that was interesting, let's get out of here," I said to someone.

In the morgue in the room next to ours, there was a child who had been killed in Willowbrook, a home for mentally handicapped children at the time. Willowbrook made the news through an investigative reporter due to their inhumane treatment of children. I don't remember if this was after the story broke. It didn't matter anymore. The only thing I could do, by this point, was watch the reality of life and death pass before my eyes—not in the news, but in the flesh. There was nothing I could do to change it except maybe give death a little bit of dignity for a proper funeral, even if it was just at Potter's Field, where the unknown John and Jane Does and the destitute are buried in New York City.

During morgue duty, I switched from White Russians to Screwdrivers. If they were going to put me in my own casket and close the lid, I was completely satisfied with that idea. I became a full-fledged alcoholic in six months. I drank enough for my entire lifetime in those six months. I wasn't alone, either. One guy in my class was such a sweetheart, a gentle soul—so unfit to be in the industry, and so not wanting to be there. He had been "reasoned" and forced into it by his family. He was caught in the act of attempting suicide one night, yet he graduated. I don't know how long he lasted in the business, but I always pray that he just walked away from it as soon as he got home. He just couldn't do it. Another guy overdosed not too long after graduation; a little later, another student from my class died of a heart attack. Whether they have grown up with it in their family or not, some people are not made to face reality on such a level, and are

unable to do good and give dignity to the human condition in this specific way.

It is said that doctors—or anyone, for that matter,
who can open a human body—lack a certain amount
of humanity. All I can say is, thank God. I have had
more than twelve operations, and that inhumanity has
saved my life more times than I ever thought would be
necessary. Just because I haven't had the ability to do
it myself doesn't mean my gratitude doesn't run deep.
Literally.

I met Erich March, from March Funeral Homes
in Maryland. He kept me sane, human, and spiritual
enough to carry on. He was married, and had a new
baby at the time. He lived with four other guys from
school in the city. Some of them were students from
another semester. They rented an apartment over a funeral home that had three floors fit for a king. Apparently, the owner had completely redone the top three
floors. One floor was a gym, another had a kitchen
and living room, and the third floor had the bed-
rooms. I never went up there, and didn't know how
large the rooms were, but I bet they weren't small, by
any means. When Erich finished school, his wife divorced him, I was told. Apparently, he was another
guy who made the mistake of thinking that things can
make up for good communication. I think that building was used for the movie *Klute*, in which Jane Fonda
supposedly rented an apartment.

Well, one day, some of us were out walking, I don't
remember where. I was in front of Erich. Sometimes,
the sidewalks get crowded, and you have to walk in
single file. I don't know what we were talking about.

I could talk to Erich about anything, but had dodged truly opening up. He said to me out of nowhere, "Laura, don't you trust me?" It stopped me in my tracks, and in a split second I had to make a decision: was I ever really going to trust anyone, ever again? I thought about it in a lightning flash, because I knew my life depended on it. Either I opened up or closed the door on life, never to open it again. I took a deep breath, jumped into the dark, and took a leap of faith. I kept an open door in order to remain honest with myself and others, and to be brave enough to expose myself to the world. This kept me alive. Erich hasn't changed a bit. We are still friends. His family still owns the majority of the funeral business in Baltimore, and is now branching out to another state. Everyone knows them in Baltimore. His whole family is in the business, and they are well-suited for it, with their generosity and ability to be there for people in need. He's an honest-as-hell kind of dude. He still paints, and put on a play not too long ago with a company he created about resurrection of the self through faith. Erich is on the radio all the time, providing food for thought so people can become more active in their communities in effective and life-changing ways. You can watch an interview with him on YouTube. He has won at least one prestigious award, and has created at least one charity to give the financially stressed the ability to afford prominent schools in Baltimore. He is smart, honest, and funny, and fears no one. Erich is one of the finest blessings I have ever received in my life. He was the one who drew depictions of teachers and situations in the McAllister yearbook that year. Not only did he capture everyone he drew, but his sketches were hysterical. He had Mr. McAllister doing the tango with the skeleton from Anatomy class.

One more thing about living in Manhattan changed me permanently. Jackie and I both needed haircuts. She looked around, and chose one of the hairstylists in a neighborhood she trusted. The owner's name was Tommy. I got my hair shaped according to its natural contours. Jackie took a chance on a whole different haircut and style. We spent a lot of time there, getting the haircuts and just talking. I liked Tommy a lot. He said, "I am going to a party that Andy Warhol is giving tonight. Do you want to go?" Jackie and I looked at each other as if to say, *How much weirder can this neighborhood get?* We both said, "Sure."

We got dressed as appropriately as we could, and met Tommy back at his shop. The party wasn't far—it was on the other side of 14th Street and Park Avenue South. We walked there. As we arrived and walked to the top of the steps, a naked man and woman were having straight-up sex on the stairs. I walked around them, saying, "Excuse me. Excuse me," and went up to the room where the party was. I knew this party was going to be an original. We didn't see whether Andy Warhol was there or not—we just had our eyes on the people.

The further Tommy and I walked into the party, the more people there were to squeeze through. At that point, I lost Jackie. Tommy was leading me further back. It actually might have been toward the front of the place. I walked straight into this one woman who was quite heavy and dressed completely in black, with chalk-white makeup and black eyeliner that made the corpses we worked on in the morgue look good. She had sparkly antennae things coming out of her teased-up hair, a drink in her hand, and her arm outstretched, talking to someone.

I didn't want to be rude or die laughing on the spot, and end up in the morgue myself from losing my breath. I thought I was scared of the morgue—I expected that—but this had it beat. I nearly jumped out of my shoes. I politely smiled and said hello, and she gave me a nod of the head as Tommy and I passed around her.

Tommy told me about his life. I liked him; I liked his honesty and vulnerability. He said, "Do you want to go back to the shop and have sex in one of the chairs?"

I thought about it. He had longer blonde hair, was good looking, and was a gentle kind of guy. I said, "No."

"Why not?" he asked.

"Because I like you."

He looked at me and said, "You frustrated nun."

I thought that was great! I had wanted to be a nun when I was young, and my father told me, "If you do, I will show you the door, and will never allow you in the house again." That really fried my nerves. I looked at Tommy and told him the story, saying, "You see, that's why I like you. I would like to get to know you much better before we do it." I was being honest. I really liked him, and I knew it would be just that night, for fun, and we would never be boyfriend and girlfriend, just better friends. I just wanted to see more deeply into him so it would be more fun.

He saw that, put his head down, and said, "I can't." I knew it was because that would expose him more than having his pants off ever could.

The party was getting more crowded, and we were getting squished. "Want to get high?" he asked.

"Sure."

"Okay, I have to go to a friend's house to pick up some pot."

I wasn't drinking anything at that party. I knew I might end up looking like the woman with the antennae permanently if someone was spiking the drinks. It was fine with me to leave the place to get fresh air. As we were walking to leave and getting closer to the steps, I began wondering if anyone else was screwing around on them. No one was. I thought, *Thank God, it's so much easier.* I didn't have to go anywhere the next day. I think because of the party, Jackie and I decided to stay in the city for the weekend instead of going home. Tommy and I left in a cab, I don't remember where. We got there and took the elevator up, and he knocked on the door. A completely naked woman opened the door, smiled, and invited us in, happy to see Tommy. I thought, *No, this isn't happening.* I said, "Hi."

Her boyfriend was sitting on the sofa with a robe on and his balls hanging out. I was not computing this scene; it was too much information for one night.

So I said, "Hi. Nice to meet you."

He said, "Want to sit down?"

I said thank you and sat down on the opposite end of the sofa, as far away as I could get. This guy was ugly. It was hard to look at him just on that alone.

I watched his girlfriend walk back in the room, still completely naked, and I turned to look at Tommy with a look that said, *Oh, so you really know these people well.* Tommy must have given a mild nod my way, because when I looked back at his friend, he had covered his privates. At the time, I was used to seeing more corpses that way than living people. He and Tommy started talking. I wasn't paying attention. I figured, *It's between them, this transaction. I might as well talk to the woman.* This time, she came back from another room with a short, light kimono on, closed.

I had seen the guy give her a look like, *We got a straight one here.* We genuinely smiled at each other. She was stoned out of her skull—on what I didn't know. They both were. Then Tommy said, "Okay, thanks, see you later." They both smiled at me. I returned it, said goodbye, and Tommy and I left the apartment.

I think I shook my head to get that memory out. Tommy said to me, "I'm sorry."

I looked at him and said, "Hey, what the hell."

We went back, but not to the party. We got off at his shop, walked the couple of blocks back to Gramercy Park, and smoked pot. It was late, and no cops were around that we saw. We gave each other a passionate kiss and said goodnight. I liked him. Too bad I didn't get to know him better. He was a nice guy who seemed to be one of the city's victims of isolation, driven nearly to madness from it. He was a sensitive guy. The kind the city liked to crush.

CHAPTER 18

Residency

WHEN I CAME HOME to the Parkside Residence, Jackie was already home. I closed the door behind me, feeling like I had run the bases and was home safe. We looked at each other and started laughing, trying to erase the images that had been burned into our minds.

I said, "Hey, did you see the woman with the white makeup and sparkly antennae?"

She said, "Yeah." Her face was like a girl from the outer reaches of Connecticut who had just walked out of a living New York City funhouse. Even I was freaked out, and the city was my home. She was freaked out completely.

While I was getting undressed to wash up and get comfortable, I said, "After I lost you, where did you go?"

"Laura, I saw things tonight so freaky, I swear I could only have been hallucinating. Do you think they put something in the drinks?"

I told her, "I don't know, because I didn't drink—I wasn't going there. All I knew was that just walking into the place was like walking into a different universe."

She never explained what else she saw . . . or if she did, I have gladly erased it from my memory banks.

We laughed a lot about the whole thing: what we expected, and what, in reality, we had experienced. Then we laughed some more. I was sad about Tommy. Jackie said she was going to sleep. I had a journal I was keeping: mostly my prayers, thoughts about God and life, some poetry and sketches. A few lines about when I was sad, etc. I was smoking cigarettes at the time, and made sure I was always awake enough to put them out. I had started reading a book when I heard the most terrified, stuttering scream. I never heard anyone scream in terror before. It was Jackie, screaming, "Lauuuura!"

I looked up across the room. She had her back to me and it looked like she was sleeping. Then I felt this coldness coming from the foot of my bed. Once it had gone up my feet and ankles, I said with all my heart, three times out loud, "Sacred Heart of Jesus, pray for us." Then I saw what looked like people, standing shoulder to shoulder to the left of me, like a wall. It wasn't scary; just a very curious thing to see. I could see rows of them, like a chorus, but I couldn't tell how many rows of people were there. I didn't see the bottom of anyone's clothing, and it appeared they were all wearing the same thing. It wasn't so much the clothes I noticed, though—it was the number of people. There was space between us. I could see all of them, and they didn't end. Nor did they say a word. I didn't see myself as one of them. The last thing I remembered, I was still in bed. From my perspective it seemed like nothing unusual. If someone were to say to you, "People standing shoulder to shoulder," what image comes to mind? Then put in rows—one row in front of the other, with no end.

Then the vision just went away, and a warmth filled the room—no cold whatsoever. It was a comforting warmth; no chills, nothing. Then I noticed I was still in bed, soaked in sweat. There was no way I could think of that it could be explained. It was a personal experience that I am not sure I can adequately describe. It was not natural; it was a supernatural experience.

Jackie sat up, and I said, "What happened?"

She said, "I once knew this guy called Feathers. The door opened and he was standing in the doorway." She was still really scared, just talking about it. She continued, "Then the door completely opened, and he started to walk in, but there was this dog with him that ran in and jumped over me. I felt its hair brush across my face, and I started to scream to you for help."

"What time is it?" I asked. What had felt like five minutes had actually been three hours. We just were stunned by all of it.

We smoked a few cigarettes and went back to sleep after a while, because we knew in our gut we were safe.

I said to myself, *Jesus, I had no idea how powerful that prayer is. I will never forget to say it when I get scared again. Thank you, thank you, thank you.* And I went to sleep.

Over forty years have passed, and I have thought about that experience. A lot has changed, and I went on to learn a lot more from school. I can neither deny nor explain it, nor can anyone else prove or disprove that experience. All I can say is, it has been food for thought for me for decades.

I did learn, through much thought, about choirs of angels. But these guys had no wings. They were just people, standing shoulder to shoulder; rows of people. I now know that anything frightening can be overcome by standing shoulder to shoulder, and anything harmful can be changed to beneficial. I know this from a completely condensed, atomic, physical experience of my own. This is the same principle as when atoms are not as physically condensed, or are vibrating at a higher frequency and are much less atomically dense.

Now, about the cold? I have heard on many fronts that that is what happens when a soul passes, and needs the energy to make its presence felt. I had never experienced that before, and I have never experienced that again. I can't say for a fact what it was, except I know that I have never gotten cold so methodically, before or afterward. Yes, it scared me into calling for help, but to someone I know. I have faith of experience that His life and warmth are stronger than any coldness. He has experienced death, but remains alive, and is benign. Just a really cool kind of guy.

But the Feathers part of it? If I look back at what I learned in school about ancient Egyptian death rituals, there is one that says that when you die, a scale is brought before you. Your heart is put on one side of a scale, and a feather on the other. If your heart is heavier than the feather, you are in trouble. What strikes me about this is the large, beautiful scale my grandfather had on a table in his funeral parlor, next to the entrance to the chapel and the upstairs. In the United States, the scales stand for equal justice. But to have them in a funeral home makes me think about whether or not I am doing justice to myself and others. Or are others doing justice to themselves? All our hearts are being weighed, even by ourselves, daily. How much does choice fall into this equation?

The dog Jackie described always got me; she had actually felt its hair. I cannot speak for her experience, nor do I intend to ever say that I know what it was, or go into any explanation about that. I accept her experience as her experience, and neither disregard nor deny it.

I do know that when I went to St. John's University to finish my bachelor in funeral service administration, I took a literature class as an optional course. There, I learned from Fr. Robert Lauder, who, I found out, was a hot-stuff author and movie critic for *The Brooklyn Tablet*, a weekly paper of Catholic topics.

Apparently, this guy just loved film like crazy. I found him so cool. I said to him, "Oh, my son's name is Robert."

He looked at me from his over-six-foot stature and said, "I'm just a bigger pain in the neck, right?"

I laughed, and said, "Yeah, you are." He made me read literature I don't normally read and don't normally like, but he was just so bright and such a nice guy, with a regular sense of humor that could bring me to tears at times from laughing.

One day, he began to talk about "the hound of God." BINGO! My brain just lit up.

I learned you cannot say what God is except in description, because when you do, He is not. Tricky son of a gun, isn't He? Look at this, I thought; *Someone who loves unconditionally, who will follow you endlessly in devotion, protect you, guide you, comfort you, save your life, care for you, and also scare the shit out of you if you don't recognize it.*

I recently heard a quote by Muriel Rukeyser: "The Universe is not made of atoms; it's made of stories." Our own, I would imagine.

After spending the summer and the rest of the school year embalming myself with drink at Pete's Tavern, graduation finally arrived. A serious relief, yet I would miss the people I had shared such a harrowing experience with.

My dad gave me some time to breathe, but now I had to serve my year of "residency," something like what a doctor has to do, then take a state board test at the end of the year. How did I spend it? Not drinking as much, by any means, but I was washing the embalming room from floor to ceiling, installing intercoms *in* the ceiling, cleaning, reorganizing the small office downstairs, painting it, and hanging up prints of old sailing ships on one full wall for "my office." Yeah, tell me another one. My dad had saved a slew of the prints because he loved them so much. I shoveled snow, washed down the hallways of both sides of the buildings, repaired anything that needed repairs that did not require someone licensed to do, cleaned the ladies' and men's rooms until they sparkled, cleaned the leather furniture, set up the rooms for funerals, and sat in on making funeral arrangements while Dad beamed as he introduced me as his daughter (I could make arrangements, but could not legally sign them yet). I could pick up death certificates after they had been made. You name it, I did it. I learned the prices of caskets and the best way to see what someone would like. I started to dress the dead and put makeup on them. I said goodbye to Goldie, and began to feel unable to breathe.

I met up with a friend, Kathy, from high school. She lived on Jane Street in the Village, and I spent every spare moment I had with her. She was working her way toward becoming an actress, taking dance classes; and she did other jobs just to make money to live on. She worked in offices, mostly. At least with her, I could breathe. On weekends, we went to yoga classes at the Yoga Institute and saw *The Rocky Horror Picture Show* at midnight. We did all kinds of fun stuff.

Then, one day, Kathy said to me, "Laura, I am dating a lawyer, Ethan, and he bought us tickets to the ballet to see Baryshnikov dance. He got seats close to the stage, and he can't go. Wanna go?"

I didn't know who Baryshnikov was. I had never been to a ballet before, so I said, "You bet!" It was New York at its sanest.

I was still drinking and smoking pot, but not enough to get really drunk, and not enough to fall unconscious so I could completely deny what I was doing. It was just enough to keep the edge off. I made a promise that I was going to do the best I could, even though this was not what I wanted to do. I wanted to be twenty going on twenty-one somewhere other than a funeral home, but by that time, I didn't know what I could be, other than that. So much of me was devoted to it by now; I lived and breathed it. I had to figure out a better way to help grieving families. Letting them just leave after the funerals felt like a shared artery had been cut. I couldn't let them just walk out so drained without any further comfort—or me, either. I needed time to think. So off to the ballet I went.

We sat very close to the stage. The place was beautiful, but honestly, all I remember of that night was the lights going down, a full orchestra playing the most beautiful music I had ever heard, and my introduction to Mikhail Baryshnikov. Young, very handsome, blonde-haired and blue-eyed, he entered the stage at what looked like six feet off the ground. I was immediately in love with ballet.

Downtown, Grandma and Grandpa had prints of Degas's ballerinas hung behind the sofa. I had looked at them all the time and dreamed on them, but this performance blew me out of my socks. I couldn't believe what I was seeing. I didn't know it was possible for men and women to be so incredibly strong and graceful. To me, a quarterback was a wuss compared to what they were physically capable of doing—and doing it so fast, for such consistent lengths of time. It took my breath away.

Afterward, we went to a restaurant in SoHo that looked out into an open garden. We were inside, as it was still a little too chilly to sit outside for Kathy. I wanted warmth, too, that night, and to smell all the different delights being served from the front of this restaurant. I had Fettuccini Alfredo for the first time, with fresh cracked pepper on top. It was so creamy and delicious. Kathy said, "Ethan said the treat is on him tonight. Order anything you want." So we had dessert and cappuccino. Oh, did I prefer this side of the face of Manhattan. That night nourished my soul and kept me going, in some small part of me, for the rest of my life. As soon as I could afford it, I was going to buy season tickets to the ballet, even if I had to eat cereal for dinner for a year. I bought them; then, after Rita taught me about opera and I was again shocked at how wonderful the stories were, I bought season tickets to the opera, as well. I was going to be kept alive if it killed me. And of course, it nearly did.

CHAPTER 19

Receiving My License to Die

I FINISHED MY RESIDENCY, stood before the State Board, answered their questions, and received my second plaque to operate. The entire funeral home was refreshed, renewed, and ready to go with an additional title on the business card and a licensed funeral director running the place. Either of us could be called, when needed, at any time of the day or night. I was proud and happy, despite it all. I was a groundbreaker in the community in more ways than one. I brought fresh air. I was young enough, pretty enough, smart enough, social enough, genuinely cared enough, and had energy enough to change the things around me. Plus, nobody thought the way I did (no surprise there). I had moved out of my parents' house by this time, to Carroll Gardens down by Union Street, where Grandpa had taken me shopping as a kid.

The apartment didn't have a stove, so I had to buy one.

I found a second-hand unit in one of the local papers. A man and his son delivered it. We got to talking, and wouldn't you know it, he had known my Grandfather Al. His face lit up with a big smile, and he said, "I am so glad this is going to you. I remember your grandfather and the bar he owned." I'd never heard before that Grandpa had owned a bar. That was a first. He just beamed, and he and his son installed the stove for me happily. I felt like I knew this guy like a friend I would have forever. It was great.

I asked my mom the next time I saw her, "When did Grandpa own a bar?"

She said, "Before the business, but it was so much work he had to close it. Grandma couldn't do so much cooking."

Dad was figuring out a way to get the tenants who were living in the apartment above the office to move out and to get me into it, so I could be there instantly when needed. I got in all right, but the exhaust from the embalming room seemed to have gone straight up through that airshaft. I couldn't get away from that stuff if I tried. I knew it wasn't used for that, and that the embalming room was on the other side of the building. But it didn't seem to matter. It was like living above a restaurant: the smells just rise. I installed an air conditioner and hoped for the best.

My dad showed me something he had inherited from his father. It was a little clicker like a child would play with—a Halloween one. It was orange, with a carved pumpkin on it and bats flying. He used it for when he and the pallbearers stood before the altar in church after the deceased's casket had been rolled before it. When it was clicked, everyone would genuflect together, then leave the church. It was all worn from all the time Grandpa had used it. Dad kept it in the desk drawer. Of course, I took it, and used it just as Grandpa had done before me. It was something of his I could still touch. It was like we were still holding hands walking down the street, like when I was a little girl. Halloween—that was Grandpa all over. He always made me smile, and reminded me that life was more than I knew, and was worth smiling about.

Halloween is actually a Catholic holy day that celebrates the Eve of All Hallows (those who are holy) and the night before All Saints Day. It is followed by the Feast of All Souls Day. Both are days of prayer, gratitude, celebration, and remembrance. Of course, the holiday was originally on a pagan day of celebration, but that is not surprising, because in reality, the Easter Bunny has no morals at all. He breeds candy bunnies like mad and without regard. He breeds endlessly with all the creativity as only an Easter bunny can. If you look closely when he is not looking, you can catch him passing around chocolate Passover coins, too. And I caught him once playing with a dreidel! The Easter Bunny has the morals of spring.

I ran my first funerals with Butch, Dad's friend who kept the business open for him. He was the hearse driver, and he was always there to back me up if needed. Things always went smoothly. We worked really well together. Butch was another lighthearted guy. He had known deep sorrow, too, but kept a twinkle in his eye. When he was young, he had been a mischievous little boy. I could see it. He told me about the "bucket of blood" bars he would go to when he was younger. We would both laugh. Not exactly my style—but wasn't it, really? He always caught me off guard with a laugh. I still find life ironic and very funny after the hurt dissipates.

With Dad, my dividing lines were drawn when I learned how to do everything on my own. His idea of making a profit on a casket was to let people who had more money pay more; that would cover the expense for people who could not normally afford a better casket. I was uncomfortable with that. I thought all caskets should be sold as is, reasonably to all, no matter what the cost. That way, no one felt they were being cheated. We would be known for being fair, and that would bring in more business; therefore, we would do a better turnover. That was when my dad realized I wasn't him, and out-and-out war began. Dad was getting better; he was fighting for his life. It was his business and it would be run his way. He told me I should do things my way as long as it was his way.

At first, it made me laugh, because he would say, "You know, Laura, you are just like Grandpa. You would give the business away." I looked at him and took it as a compliment, because I knew how many people had loved Grandpa for his gentleness. To me, it didn't mean there weren't things that I saw more clearly than my dad. Times were changing, and things were becoming softer. And softer makes for better business. A win-win situation will always work better than a dog-eat-dog contest.

There was no explaining it. This was where his stroke started to affect me and the business. He started to take it personally. If he didn't approve of the way I saw things and wanted to move on it, he started calling me stupid. "You don't know anything, or how to run anything the right way." Trying to bring the business forward became like walking in quicksand.

Then it started weighing on me. I was twenty-one, almost twenty-two, and I was starting to see only black. One day, Dad was sitting in the office where the lights were to all the chapels, and he called, "Laura, there is a body in Chapel B that needs to be dressed. Do it." That was fine, because that was my job. I had just come up from downstairs and walked into the chapel, waiting for him to put the lights on so I could see what I was doing. There was always a time constraint, so commands were totally acceptable; they told you how much time you had left to finish what you needed to do in the best way possible. Hearing them meant the family was coming to see their loved one. Once they were there, the fewer things that needed to be changed, the better, because it could be upsetting to someone. That was to be avoided at all costs.

The lights were still off. I couldn't see anything. I walked up to where the casket should be, then scanned the chairs where usually the person's clothes would normally be waiting. Instead of clothes, I saw a dead baby, with clothes on the seat next to it.

The lights still hadn't been turned on. I didn't know why—maybe he couldn't get up fast enough. Being paralyzed made it easy for him to quickly lose his balance, to the point of falling. Things took a lot longer than if I had done them. I picked up the baby, and just held it in my arms. I had never dressed a baby before. I turned ice cold inside in the dark.

Then Seb, the embalmer, came to the door. He must have just finished embalming the baby. He looked at me in the dark, and said, "Laura, are you alright?" I wasn't, and he knew I wasn't. "If you can't do it, I'll come in and do it for you."

His genuine concern for me gave me the strength to know that this may have been the first time I would do this, but it certainly wouldn't be the last. I looked back at him in gratitude, and said, "No Seb, I can do it."

He said, "Okay," and left. Before I knew it, the lights were turned on, and I started to dress the baby.

I didn't know what to do with this child. There was no "coochy, coochy, koo." There was no "Don't cry, honey." There was nothing. I put the baby on my lap and dressed it as gently and as tenderly as I could. Thinking of the baby, I was trying to stay alive inside enough to be able to somehow comfort the mother, if that was at all possible. I didn't even know where I could begin. I finished, and walked into the office.

I don't remember anything about what happened next except that the family came in. I don't even remember if I brought the mother to the chapel, or Dad did, or what. I couldn't bear it. All I remember seeing was the back of that woman with her friend holding her up, sobbing from a hole so deep inside—an emptiness so complete, it seemed eternal. Her friend was taking her downstairs, either to the ladies' room, where she could put some cold water on her face, or to just sit and cry, out of sight of everyone.

Apparently, after that, it was my job to dress the dead babies because I was a woman. And for some other reason, it seemed that all the babies who died in the area came to our funeral home. It was always Middle Eastern children who had died from the Sudden Infant Death Syndrome. The cause was a medical mystery. For decades, the medical community could not understand why babies would just die in their cribs. Guess what? It still is. It is considered rare, but I can tell you that it happens more than you realize. It happens during sleep, mostly, when a baby is anywhere from two to four months old.

That did me in. The thought of just dying myself seemed a lot easier than being alive. I was running funerals from a local church, Our Lady of Lebanon. Monsignor Shaheen was the priest who ran it. He would always come to our funeral home to say the Final Prayers at night, before the funeral. He called me "Gloria" in his Lebanese accent: "Gloria, Gloria." One time, I had to call the Rectory, and the woman who cared for it answered. When I told her who was calling, she said, "Oh, Gloria." Just so sweet. He had a sharp eye, too, and had been watching me dying inside and just getting sick.

Sick from the smell of death and embalming fluid and dead flowers, day after day. Business was increasing more and more. I cared, and I cut people a break, but I was seriously beginning not to want to go on anymore.

Monsignor Shaheen showed up one day, and sat down in the upstairs office with me and Dad, just for a visit and chat. He said, "Our church is going to Rome for five days in the fall to be a part of the celebration of one of our monks into sainthood. Laura, would you like to go with us?"

There was no way in hell this old priest wasn't going to stop bending my father's arm until he said yes. My father knew it, and so did I. I looked at my dad; he knew he had no choice, so he said yes. Joanne had always wanted to see Europe for as long as I could remember, so I piped up with, "Can I bring my sister, too?" He said, "Yes, of course you can. She would be more than welcome. Bring her, and your father will pay for it." I thought, *I had better run for the hills before Dad smiles at him and kills me.* Dad laughed, and said okay. But the old cheapo only paid for our airfare.

I told Joanne as fast as I could. She said she would be willing to quit her job, if necessary, to stay more than five days; she wanted to see Greece. I asked Monsignor Shaheen if we could do that. He said, "Gloria, you stay as long as you want. See as much as you want, and I will make your father agree to it." That was all he had to say.

Get away from death, breathe fresh air, see something different, go on an adventure? *Hell, yeah.* We started in Greece, then drove west from Rome until we got to Holland. Five weeks. My desire to live and breathe, to see and think outside of the darkness and not be criticized, was taking hold. I was beginning to live again. I was beginning to feel as light as air. I did what I needed to do with more energy, and without falling into such a deep depression that I would find myself unable to move. In other words, my ol' buddy showed up from a completely unexpected place to rescue me again. What can I say, or could I say, but "Thank you, God," especially when He was being so blatant about it this time.

CHAPTER 20

Getting My Wings

IT WAS A TIME TO REMEMBER. We slept in guesthouses, rented a cheap little car, and traveled the back roads, where we met people outside the cities. We did visit the sights, but I had had enough of the city. I needed fresh air and calm people.

Greece was wonderful. We stayed in a family hotel at the foot of the Parthenon. Joanne had been a Philosophy major, and I guess she had expected more of the place. She was disappointed, but for me, it was a striking spiritual experience. When we had been there for five days, I felt the energy and experience of Christ palpably. We took a boat ride to see different islands. The fresh air and sun just made me relax and unwind. I was still like a tightly wound coil, but the Greek wine was uncoiling me nicely. It was wonderful.

We flew to Rome. We stayed in a modest hotel, and upon seeing the history of Rome the centuries had built, one on top of the other, I threw up. Literally.

Way, way too much overwhelm. The Coliseum was closed for repairs, and the Trevi Fountain was being washed, so no coins. It was a small disappointment, but I didn't care. There was no embalming fluid to be had anywhere, though we did see a funeral. It was the procession of a casket being taken out of someone's home. I was transported a hundred years back. Nothing had changed since my great-grandfather's time. Nothing. The casket was just a pine box, shaped like the ones in old western movies. I said to myself, *Of course I'd have to run into a funeral*, but upon looking back now, I could see how it had been in Great-grandpa's time. I was there. I met Monsignor Shaheen's nephew, and fell so deeply in love, it was as if he was as much a part of me as my own blood. Living without him, I could never be whole. His name was George, and he was becoming a doctor in Paris. One night, we were all at the dinner table, and Monsignor Shaheen told someone to put the wine bottle in front of me. He said, "I like you when you're drunk." I thought, *Oh, God!!* Believe it or not, that was what gave me permission within my own soul to stop drinking. I could face all of it, everything, stone cold sober. Just not then.

I saw the pope, and St. Peter's Square, and the Pieta (behind bulletproof glass). All Joanne did was complain, "If the Catholic Church sold all the works of art they have, they could feed all the poor." She thought God had cut out on her. I knew how she felt, but by that time, I still had to rely on my ol' buddy, like it or not. It was what it was. The sainthood procession was very spiritually touching, as you could see and feel how many people loved the old monk.

Joanne wanted to see the Spanish Steps, so we went there. I was enthralled, but the traffic and the people of the city were not clean air and open space. That was what I needed. I was becoming ill from all the chemicals I had been breathing in. I had been inside more often than not, and had had enough smog and car exhaust at home. We spent about five days in Rome, and decided to stay with George in Paris when we arrived there.

Florence was the next stop. It was beautiful. We spent most of our time in the museums, and just walking around. The food and the beauty of the place were wonderful: very old, but not as congested as Rome. We were told it was more of a college town. I remember an outdoor café, and the cappuccino I had there. I felt the stress just begin to melt. I bought most of my gifts in Florence. I couldn't believe where I was. What was I doing in Europe? It had to be some kind of dream. It was as if I had to pinch myself every step of the way. I had never met a more magnanimous man than Monsignor Shaheen. He sent me away from the heartache and helplessness to figure out how to have a real effect on the families. I had to learn how not to cry, to detach so far. Otherwise, I would have cried myself completely useless, or grown too cold out of sheer survival. This was a way for me to be detached and distracted safely from all of it, and still let it work itself out in me. I was so grateful. It was centuries of artwork. It just fed my soul.

We took a train to Venice and got off outside the city. We rented a car and found a small family hotel. They only spoke Italian, of course, but we managed. They had a lion cub in their backyard, fenced in. I didn't know enough Italian, and neither did Joanne, to ask why. They did let us play with him. Don't play with a lion cub unless you want to have him try to carry you off by the top of your head, or at least crush it for fun. Sweet little puss, could he know his own strength? Come to think of it, what was that? Because we didn't get to see the Coliseum, we were able to get a little taste of it? I didn't know, and it was okay. Talk about getting a taste of history. Ouch.

We were living on bread, cheese, and wine. I preferred the wine, with only bread. I had to develop a taste for cheese over time. We spent my birthday in Venice, and took a gondola ride to see the sights, like the Bridge of Sighs. Apparently, it was the last bridge people went under before they went to prison. I loved Venice; something in me could relate to it. For me, being human, with all its complexity, was getting to be a puzzle with a prison hidden inside. I seemed to be locked in it, too. It wasn't comfortable working my way out of it, but this certainly was making it easier. Venice was simple, the sights were beautiful, the people were warm and welcoming, and the weather wasn't scorching hot; it was cooler and more comfortable. I could live with that, and it made it easier to think about which end of the business I wanted to focus on. Did I have to work with the corpses, or could I take it in another direction, and move away from that? Learn what was available?

That night, we had dinner in the dining room in our hotel. There was a group of Italian guys who had just won a karate championship there, and they were celebrating. They sang "Happy Birthday" to me. I said to God, *Man, I am trying to leave Brooklyn and bad memories for a while. Can't you cut me a break?*

He said, "*No, because you are going home, let's remember that. No hundred percent forgetting, you know that, not until you make peace with it.*"

I said something like, "*Grrrrrr.*" I got as drunk as a skunk, and the waiter had his eye on me. A very handsome Italian. No English, though. We managed to communicate clearly by making love the whole night. It was great. We were leaving the next morning, and he had taken off his cross and put it on the end table. I didn't see him before Joanne and I left, but I handed it back to his mother. Oooh, she was not happy with me. But I left him in the hands of God, hopefully to realize that if she killed him, he would go straight to heaven. He deserved it.

We said good bye to little Lione, the lion cub, and left for Germany. The road was blocked for some reason, so we had to go around. We ended up in Communist Yugoslavia. Oh, Lord. We got stopped by two armed guards with rifles attached to their sides. "Uh-oh," I said.

Joanne said something like, "Holy shit!" as she had to pull off to the side. I could tell they had already used the rifles, and wouldn't hesitate a second to use them again. They went through everything; made us open the trunk, and they combed through every inch of it. One of the guards saw I had my white bathrobe with my sneakers perched on it. It was dirty laundry.

He looked at it and said, "Mmmmf, Americano." I didn't say a word—just held my breath. We got back into the car. Joanne said, "Thank God we came out of that alive, and especially that there wasn't any pot in the car." They gave the car one more look-over to see if maybe they had missed a spot, but there was nothing to arrest us for. We drove out of there without breaking the speed limit.

"Think they did that just to scare us?" I asked.

"I don't know," Joanne replied, "but the faster we get out of here, the better." I had never agreed with my sister more.

We had to go through the Black Forest at night, and they call it the Black Forest for a very good reason. Don't ask me how we kept to the road—it was so dark, we could only see as far as our little headlights could go. I was the co-pilot reading the map. All of a sudden, the road opened up to a fully-lit chalet: a restaurant, with rooms above. It was like a dream after deep, nightmare-filled sleep: all carved wood inside with comforting low lights and antlers over the doorways. It was so expensive and warm and cozy. We had beer and Cordon Bleu.

We had put money aside to splurge on a good hotel so we could take a real shower, clean up, sleep in a comfortable bed, and start fresh. Well if this wasn't it, it didn't exist. The comforter on the bed was over a foot thick with down feathers. After being in Communist Yugoslavia for only half an hour, this was a come-to-Jesus moment. We stayed just one night, but we left cleaner and more rested than we had ever been in our lives. I loved Bavaria. I had never seen such green grass, with shepherds herding sheep on mountains that went straight up. It defied gravity.

We spent a day in Berlin, but again, I was so well-rested, I don't remember it. I was beginning to come back into my own skin again. Considering all the times I had jumped out of it, I was doing pretty good.

Joanne and I drove through the Italian Alps and the Swiss Alps. In the Italian Alps, we ran into a man with a scar across his face, from his forehead to his lip. He wanted to talk to me. I had never rolled up a car window so fast, and told Joanne to hightail it out of there. He scared the hell out of me. The rest of the ride through the Alps was almost unreal. The height and depth of the mountains were hard to take in. We were driving above the clouds. Boy, did that put some space inbetween me and my so-called office. It was only called my office because I had become the corporate secretary, and did all the billing and correspondence. Otherwise, Dad claimed the chair behind the desk. That was okay; he hadn't been that happy in years.

We arrived in Switzerland and met a truly nice older couple who had been traveling, as well. We talked about what we had seen, what they had seen, and what there was left to see. It was so nice. And it was wonderful staying in people's homes as we traveled from place to place. Not one was a funeral home. My body was recognizing the memory.

We drove through France and north to Paris, where we stayed with George. He was working during the day, so we did all the sightseeing we wanted. At night, we went out to dinner together. Joanne's friend from home, who was Asian, had a brother living in Paris. Joanne had promised to look him up, so she did. He was a tall, nice guy—very polite. He got really upset when he found out where we had bought our perfume. He said, "I wish you had spoken to me first. You were taken in by a tourist trap, and paid at least twice as much." We looked at each other. There was nothing we could do at that point. It was already done. He came out to dinner with us, and George invited another friend. The friend didn't like me. He was so rude. I looked at Joanne's friend's brother as if to say, *Should I lay this guy out?* He shook his head no, so I didn't say a word, and let him rant about how terrible Americans were. All I thought to myself was, *Laura, the guy is a jerk. We are in a nice restaurant, be nice,* as I was huffing and puffing in frustration—politely, of course, otherwise I would have proven his point quite admirably. Nobody said anything. We just waited for him to shut up.

Joanne and I took a walk down the Left Bank, where an art market had been set up that day. I bought the most beautiful painted mirror depicting a girl holding a basket of flowers. It was dream-like. I carried it home from Paris, and to this day, I carry it wherever I go. It still hangs on one of my walls.

Of course, I got to know George better. I just happened to have left my heart and breath in his.

Joanne and I traveled through Belgium and up to the Hook of Holland. We were on the last leg of our trip.

It was raining terribly one night, and we skidded into the car in front of us in Boom, Belgium. We got out in the pouring rain. Upon investigation, we discovered that we had smashed into a doctor's car. I don't know how much damage there was to his Mercedes (everyone drove a Mercedes there.) He brushed it off when Joanne offered to exchange information. We couldn't believe how nice he was, and left him with many well wishes as we drove off. Our car's bumper now wore a crooked smile.

I was too depressed, at this point, to get excited about seeing anything. I knew that everything was for the last time. I was just waiting for the last three days to end in Holland. I had never before walked up a vertical flight of steps and called them just regular steps, as they were in Holland. They were terrifying . . . especially when attempting to carry a suitcase. Amsterdam is a city of bridges, too. So calming. Of course, it was also busy, but I didn't even want to see how busy it was. I was going back to New York City. I wanted to see waterfalls and windmills and ducks, so we did.

Joanne was tired, too. Both of us were. We had known how long we would be away, and now our energy was spent. We had more things to carry home than we came with, and didn't even have enough money for two headsets to watch the movie on the plane. When we brought our little crooked-smiled car back to the rental place, we figured it was going to cost an additional arm and a leg, but they, too, brushed it off. We left happy, with kind memories.

I arrived home so much more refreshed, but honestly, no matter how much history and beauty I had witnessed, it was not the United States. The energy was not the same. When we got home, I wanted to kiss the ground, but it ended there. I still needed more time away. I didn't know how I was going to manage or where I was going to go, but one month had not made up for three years of being infused with death.

I can't say that everyone who goes into the business as a funeral director is like me. Most are skilled with a scalpel, and consider that just as important as being with the family. It isn't that way with me. With everybody I dressed, I could tell who died having lived a full life, and who had died with their talents and gifts unrealized. Some people were highly spiritual, and some—actually, most—weren't. Most were greatly loved; others were not.

Some funerals were celebratory of the person's life. At that time, people did not put pictures of their loved ones out. There was no playing of music the person had loved. It was silent and bare. The only things that were creatively expressed were the flower arrangements. The only music that was played was at Middle Eastern funerals, where a lot of the time, they paid for wailing women.

It was so culturally different from an Italian funeral. There, you didn't have to pay anyone, and the tension between wives and lovers was palpable. Certainly not all the time, of course. The difference at a Muslim funeral was that women sat separately from the men. The men went to the smoking lounge downstairs, and made a circle in front of my office. I respected their custom, but it drove me nuts. How could I get into the office without being disrespectful? Then it started to piss me off, because I wasn't even being acknowledged, except by the man who had made the arrangements, and he mostly spoke to my father. I thought, *Wait, you mean to tell me I went through that hell of embalming school, and I'm not welcome in the embalming room? For any reason?* I got mad. The ridiculous part was that I had never really wanted to be in the embalming room, but it was the principle of the matter. All they did was wash the body and say prayers over it, similarly to the Jewish tradition.

One day, we had a funeral, and the men were downstairs washing a body. I was upstairs in the office with my dad when one of the men came up to the office and asked my father, "Could your daughter come down to the embalming room?" He said the deceased man wanted to see me. I must have blinked about ten times. I couldn't have just heard what I thought I heard.

My dad said, "Ask her."

By this time, I was probably still blinking. Very humbly, the man said to me, "He wants to see you."

I still wasn't sure I was hearing correctly. I said, "Excuse me?"

"He wants to see you," the man repeated.

I said okay and followed him to the embalming room.

We were quiet. He didn't speak to me, and I thought, *Well, now, this is different.* I wasn't going to be disrespectful and go fully into the embalming room with them, so I stood at the door, not far away. The man walked in and stood next to the deceased man's head. The other man was standing on the other side, and the sheet was pulled up to the dead man's neck.

Before saying hello to the gentleman, I asked, "What did he die of?"

The man who had come for me upstairs said, "He was stabbed forty times."

I nodded my head in acknowledgement of the way he had passed. I said to the dead man, "Hey, what's up?"

I guess he didn't want to freak everyone out, because he didn't say anything. I figured I would listen and see if I got any impressions of what he wanted to say, but I heard nothing. In my silence, I looked right at his face, and promised, "I will pray for you for as long as I live." There was complete silence. I said, "Okay," turned, and went back upstairs. My dad didn't say a word, as if this stuff was nothing unusual. He was just reading his paper. I certainly didn't say anything, either, as I was so sad the man had had such a violent death. He could have used some tenderness. The two men came back up to say goodbye, and my dad took it from there.

Well, I thought that man was really nice. He was the only one besides the man who had made the arrangements who not only fully acknowledged me, but was respectful enough to invite me into my own embalming room. I don't care if anyone believes me or not, or tries to figure that one out. All I can say is, keep quiet, and join me in silent acknowledgment of another human being who suffered a violent death. Be grateful if you never do. I certainly will be.

The roof started to leak not too long after that, but Joanne was dating a roofer. His friend Dan had just come back from Kinshasa, capital of the Democratic Republic of the Congo in Africa. He had been in the Peace Corps for a year, and had just come back to the States. Born in North Dakota, he was a blonde-haired, blue-eyed cowboy. Holy cow, I was a cowgirl in my dreams. I thought I would never see George again, and figured that was something I would have to live with. I had been dating an Israeli commando

Joanne had introduced me to, but I just didn't like the guy. But my God, try to shake off an Israeli commando. It's not as easy as it sounds.

Meanwhile, Dan had a motorcycle, and I had no problem riding with him on it. It was so much fun. We went camping and did some light whitewater rafting. I was surprised to see how well he knew the night sky. We looked at the stars, and he pointed them out to me. Of course, I had no clue what he was pointing to. The sky happens to be big and busy, with a lot of stars on a clear night.

All of a sudden, I saw this machine passing by. "What's that?" I asked.

"A satellite," he replied. I thoroughly freaked out. It was like Big Brother looking down on us. I could never look at the sky again without knowing those suckers are out there. He told me recently that he sits on his porch in North Dakota and watches the space station pass by. We have remained friend for about forty years now.

In the meantime, the commando guy asked me if I wanted to go to a restaurant in the city where there was just one table. The restaurant was closed to the public, and only people who were invited had dinner. You just waited to see what they served. Oh, my God, from beginning to the end, it was wonderful, with delicious wines served with different courses. I was relaxed, and just had such a pleasant time. Everyone at the table enjoyed the food. The whole experience was delicious. So this guy and I got on the train to come home. I was snuggled on his arm, and when we looked at each other, he said to me that I smelled like a French whore.

At that point, I thought, *I never liked this jerk from the beginning. Why am I even spending another minute with him?* I figured being nice and honest, and telling him, "I don't want to go out with you, I don't like you," wasn't getting me anywhere, so I had to get mean. It was the only language he really understood.

Being molested, I found out years later, sends both women and men down a road of drug addition, alcoholism, and promiscuity. I didn't mind the promiscuity so much. Actually, after you had picked up as many dead men as I had, picking up someone warm certainly didn't hurt the situation. I had no problem with it. He was the only guy I ever went out with who embarrassed me just by being himself. After that, I thought, *If this guy hears that I am being honest with him and doesn't get it, I will just start going out with Dan, and treat him like shit.*

After Europe, I had to keep talking to living people who would keep me interested, so I went back to college at night. One of the required classes was Speech. I happened to have my mother's car one night. I don't know why, but I did. I was running late, because it took longer than the time given to find a parking space. Brooklyn is brutal in that way, unless you have your own parking. I finally found a space in front of the school. I really lucked out. I gathered my stuff together, slammed the car door, and immediately realized I had locked the keys in the car.

I found myself in a bit of an upset. I didn't know what to do first, so I decided I would go into class, and explain to the teacher what had happened and that I would be a little late. I said hello to her, and said, out of breath, "I'm late because I locked my keys in the car."

"Could you repeat that, please?" she asked. I said sure. She said, out loud, "Class, class, be quiet." Everyone settled down, and then she said to me, "Will you please repeat what you just said to me?" I shrugged my shoulders and said to the class, "I locked the keys in my car." She said, "Class, now this is how you do not speak." I said to myself, *Oh, shit, Aunt Camy reincarnated.* My Brooklyn accent was not serving me well tonight. She told me, "Come back when you get your car keys out." I just slowed down after that.

I walked out of the school, and somehow found a guy who had a hanger in his car. He got the driver's side door open. Very nice guy. I thanked him, and as I walked back into that school, I told myself I was going to ace that class. And I did.

Dan was going back home to North Dakota, but before that, his niece was getting married in Colorado, and he asked me if I wanted to go. The commando guy asked me to go somewhere with him, too. I told my father, and he said, "If you go with Dan, I will pay the airfare."

I just laughed, and said, "You got it."

"Let's go," I told Dan. He showed me how to pack lightly, and off we went. School had ended, and we left for Colorado.

I told the commando, "You don't like it? Too bad, leave." Being jaded never helped my tender heart, and this guy wasn't helping any.

We ended up driving from Colorado to North Dakota, sightseeing, having fun, swimming, and meeting different family members along the way. I loved Dan's family. His niece ended up visiting in New York. Dan taught me how to shoot a .32 rifle and a shotgun. I was good at cans and bottles, but when I heard birds above, all of a sudden, the gun in my hands went up, and I had them in my sights. I just stopped. I couldn't believe I had just done that. I had never killed anything before. Where had that come from? Dan saw me, and said, "You're just like my sister. She cried when I shot a rabbit." Target practice was so much fun, though; that shotgun threw me back about a foot.

Dan's dad had an old horse-drawn buggy that was still serviceable. They also had two horses, and his dad invited me out in it. Dan said to be careful of his dad, that he was tough on people, and if he didn't like me, not to take it personally. His father and I fell in love with each other at first sight. Dan told me his dad took the buggy out on holidays, when there were parades in town. I got in the buggy, and he drove. It was so nice. Then he handed the reins to me, and I floored it. I had those horses galloping back to the property. The poor guy was holding on for dear life. It was great. Once he had grabbed the reins back, he told me to take the harnesses off the horses and put them back in their stalls. I didn't know how the tack worked, but I eventually succeeded in pulling off the bridles and harnesses after locating the proper buckles. Dan took me to a family member's house. The horses had been in the barn a while, and were frisky. They decided everyone was going for a ride. Sure, why not? Bareback, Dan? Sure, why not? When my horse decided to jump a fence at a full gallop, I wasn't going for it. I wasn't going to break my neck just because he wanted to jump and show me who was boss. I pulled the reins back as hard as I could, and when we got up to the fence, the horse stopped dead in his tracks.

I went flying off. Even my glasses went flying. I knew if I didn't get the reins fast, my horse would take off. I jumped up as soon as I hit the ground, ran after him, got the reins, and lightly punched him in the neck. "Who's running who?" I said to him. He put his head down and walked back with me like a gentleman. I had lost my glasses.

I baled hay with Dan's brother, and experienced a violent thunderstorm the night before I was leaving. Lightning extended from one end of the sky to the other. The lights went out, and for the first time, I felt scared by nature. Dan's dad, brother, and nephew had all been struck by lightning and survived it. His dad showed me the shirt he had been wearing at the time. It was burned, with a big part of it missing. They had been putting up fencing, and somehow got hit and lived through it. How could you not love people as tough as that? Dan's dad whittled, and his mom worked with a special needs child. His dad whittled utensils for the child so he would be able to eat on his own. I loved all of them, and still treasure Dan and his soldier son, stunning daughter, horses, and land. Nothing like being able to see it all from a satellite. The best thing about being with them then was that Dan told them I was from New York. They teased me like crazy. I teased them right back, and we all laughed—but they said they couldn't tell where I was from, because I didn't have a New York accent!

Not long after, I was talking to my friends from high school, and was invited out to California for a week or so. Dad was getting upset with me about my travels, but I was going to be fully back to myself, whether he liked it or not. It was the only way I could come back with full strength and keep on going. During that whole year, the most I was gone was about two months total. After that, I went nowhere for thirty-five years.

My last trip was to California to see my friends Jacob and Hanna. The jacket I had embroidered had worn out by that time, so I embroidered him another one during my time there. They lived in Orange County, and I flew into Los Angeles. As we drove up the West Coast Highway, I saw Hearst Castle and Big Sur. I also went down to San Diego on my own for a night. We went to Tijuana and Malibu. I think it was in Malibu that I wanted to smoke some pot, so I asked Jacob if anyplace on the beach had a reputation for it. He said, "Yeah," and showed me where it was. I waited and looked around to see if anyone looked like they might be selling.

There was this good-looking guy in a van. I approached him and asked if he was selling any. He said he didn't have any on him, but he knew where he could pick some up at a friend's house. He said, "Get in the van, and we'll go."

I said, "Sure."

He was really cute. After we had driven for a while, he said, "You know, I could rape you."

I said, "You know, you wouldn't have to. I think you are really cute."

He looked at me in shock. And about five minutes later, he said, "My friend is not home. I am taking you back."

I thought to myself, *Poor guy, I scared him.* I said, "You know, we could at least exchange addresses and write to each other."

He replied, "No, I just broke up with a girl, and I don't want to get involved."

"You sure?"

"Yeah."

"Okay," I said, "but I am disappointed."

He said, "That's okay, you're in New York, and I'm here, so it would be difficult, anyway."

"You're right."

By that time, we were back, and we said goodbye.

"Did you get what you wanted?" Jacob asked.

"I didn't even get a joint."

"Too bad."

"Yeah." After that last hurrah, I left for home.

CHAPTER 21

Crash Landing

I HAD BEEN WORKING between all the trips. Each time I came back, Dad and I could always talk, but now I wanted to do what I wanted to do, and I was standing on my own. I felt rested, and able to run full steam ahead, which was what Dad had wanted from the beginning. He wanted to make up for all the money he had lost during his illness.

I ran ninety-eight percent of the funerals. I put every person in their casket, and if makeup or shaving was required, I did it. I put all the obituaries in the papers, ordered all the prayer cards, and made arrangements for church services, both in the evening for final prayers and the next day, for final services. I made the arrangements with the cemeteries, signed and picked up death certificates, and did all the billing. I ran all the cremations and washed the steps, from the first floor to the top floor on both sides of the building. I swept in front of the business and shoveled snow when necessary. I cleaned the bathrooms, and made repairs.

I was on call 24-7. If there was trouble with the boiler, I was up all night, waiting for Dad to come. If I could repair it, I repaired it. If not, I called for help, and stayed with Dad until they were finished. He would go back to Mill Basin, and I would go upstairs. The next morning, I made sure all the radiators were bled. I was there to help pick up the deceased from their homes.

I ran the funerals for the rich and the poor, Greeks, Syrians, Palestinians, Lebanese, Saudi Arabians, Italians, Irish, Puerto Ricans, Ukrainians, Catholics, Protestants, Jews, Muslims, African Americans, and Native Americans. You get the point.

Once, we had a very upper-class funeral from Brooklyn Heights. Dad wasn't sure if I should go it alone or not, so we both went. I never chew gum, but that morning, I had a craving like I'd never had before in my life. Everything was going well with the three of us: Dad, me, and the woman who made the arrangements, who Dad said was integral and important to the Heights. As the services were going on inside, the three of us stood outside talking. Then she looked at me with an Aunt Camy look. "Are you chewing gum?"

With a loud gulp, I swallowed it, looked her straight in the eye, and said, "No." I started laughing, and she looked at my dad. He had his head down, shaking it, but he was grinning. Later, Dad said, "She told me that was when she really started to like you." She was a sweetheart, no matter how stern she appeared.

The only thing I didn't do was buy the caskets, but I would sit with Dad and choose which ones I thought would work. The ones we agreed upon were the ones we bought. Dad had known the guys who sold caskets for years; it was his pleasure to do business with them.

When we disagreed, it was a schism. Of course, we disagreed about the way I sold things, but that was tolerable; there was no way he was stopping me, and it brought in more business because it was working. When it came to bookkeeping, though . . . oh, God, what a pain. He said, "I want you to take accounting courses."

"Why?" I responded. "The accountant has been using the wrong Social Security number for me for years, and you won't let me near them to change it. I am not wasting my time." He only got angrier.

That got to him, but it would have been considered suicide if I said what I wanted to say to him. One day, we were discussing the way things were changing with burials. He didn't want to hear it, because he thought it would never change. I told him, "I want to be buried like a religious Jew or Muslim. I want to be washed as prayers are said over me, wrapped in a sheet, and put into a wooden casket with no metal and dove-tailed wood."

I thought Dad was going to lunge out of his seat and pin me by the neck two feet off the ground. He became red in the face, and said, "DON'T YOU KNOW YOU'RE ITALIAN?!"

I wanted to say, "If I don't, it's because of you, going into a funeral business with so many different people and nationalities being buried." I would have had an Italian funeral in two minutes, concrete vault and all.

I was recently talking about the subject with my friend Phyllis, the same one who introduced my Thanksgiving turkey as Tom from Chernobyl. I told her, "You know, Phyllis, I think I might want to be buried in a reef. They mix your ashes in with a kind of concrete shaped like a bell or stone, and they drop you in a reef, so you can take part in making the reefs healthier."

She looked at me funny, and said, "What is that, Laura? *Reefer Madness?*"

Dad was happy with the way the business was going; it was well on its way to doubling. I knew what it took to be a full-fledged undertaker. Every time I went out to relax, I was called back by another funeral.

I still needed time-outs, and discotheques were all the rage. I liked to dance, so that was fine with me. I went I think twice. Joanne asked me if I wanted to go with her once. I did, and met a fellow named Pat, the only Italian guy I ever dated for more than ten minutes. The Italian guys usually thought I should behave a certain way, and know my place. Yeah, right. But Pat was different. He didn't want to get married, just to be lifelong friends—and so we are. The guy has a photographic memory, and never ceases to amaze me. He sent me an email asking if I remembered our first date. At first, I didn't. I don't think I wanted to remember all of it. He reminded me.

We went for a walk on the Promenade, then back to my apartment, where I was promptly called to go help with picking up a body. Pat, my date, went with me. He remembered it was in August, because he remembered the terrible smell. He said I asked him to stand on the other side of the body in case it fell for some reason, getting in the car or whatever. He got home sometime early Sunday morning. What a way to spend a first date. I asked him why he ever dated me. *I* wouldn't have dated me. I tell you, there are some really caring people out there, who no matter what are willing to show the deceased respect. He never complained once. Nice guy.

Honestly, though, I was getting tired. I was twenty-five by now, and couldn't keep on in the same way. I had to do something different, so I decided to give a seminar. I found a place called the Shell of Hope. A psychologist and a nun addressed the faith end of things, though there were people of many different faiths there.

I had a friend who knew how to make up a professional flyer, and he put it together for me. Rabbi Potasnik, who I'd met at a Jewish funeral we had, introduced me to a guy who owned a diner who was willing to donate coffee and cakes. His young daughter had died, and if he could ease the pain of someone else, he was willing to do anything he could. I went to every funeral home in the neighborhood and offered them all the information I had, in case they wanted to offer the same service to the people who came to them. They were all very polite to me, especially the guy whose clients, let's say, tended to die as a result of "lead poisoning," i.e., the Mafia.

It didn't matter. A loss is a loss, and comfort is comfort, and this had nothing to do with competition. I was working very hard on it, advertising in the local paper and posting flyers where I thought it would be appropriate.

During this time, I walked into the office one day, and my dad was there. I sat down and relaxed a bit. Dad was reading his paper, and was quiet, as usual. Then he looked up at me and said, "I had a visitor today."

"Yeah? Who?"

He said, "The Mafia guy who runs the funeral home further down."

"Yeah?"

"Do you know what he told me?"

"No," I said.

"He told me, 'Leo, your daughter has balls.'"

At that moment, I became as close to a son as he was ever going to get. I think I made my dad proud.

Rabbi Joseph Potasnik, from the neighborhood, is just the warmest guy you would ever want to meet: a people person who became president of the New York Board of Rabbis, and is now senior vice-president. He has a radio show and a television show, and was the rabbi for 9/11. He had the local paper interview me. What a *mensch*.

I was out there, pretty cutting edge, and a bit of a phenomena—but Dad was getting really, I don't know, I think it was hurt inside. I had doubled the business, but in reality, it wasn't him who had done it. He didn't commit suicide, but I think he wanted to die, because he couldn't even walk safely without dragging the right side of his body. I had gone back to school and my mind was pretty sharp, but that stroke had just broken his brain. I had energy, and he was getting older. The only thing he was really serious about was managing the money. It was a hot subject between us. He wanted me to take over, but at the same time, with all his heart, he didn't. At this point, I would have taken over, but I really didn't want to, because I wasn't free to run it the way I saw best. I was getting burned out, and his insults and digs were not making things any easier. He wanted to work, but couldn't—bottom line.

The night came for the seminar, and the weather was horrendous. It was the kind of rainstorm that only made you come out in it if you had somewhere important to go. We had a nice-sized group of people. We discussed topics like how no one can tell you how long you should grieve; you grieve as long as you grieve, but don't get consumed by it. If people just said "I am sorry for your loss," it would make it so much easier. It is better to share about the good times when you can. The seminar covered losing children, faith, the consequences of losing someone, the necessity of therapy, and avoiding shame.

It was good. I got feedback from it. One couple had lost their child and the wife told me how much the seminar helped; another woman told me how cathartic it was for her, and how grateful she was. It was a very personal experience for everyone. I had a book for comments, as well. I thought I would tweak the seminar each time I ran one, until it became an addition to the business. That way, the business could offer more of the kinds of funerals people were becoming interested in, without having it be considered anything but okay. This would make it so much more of a community experience than an isolated one. I was very happy the whole neighborhood had become a part of my effort. We pulled it off, and it was appreciated. As the last person walked out, Dad and I were leaving, too. There was still a flyer on the glass door. He ripped it off with one hand, saying, "I'm glad this shit is over with." There was no fighting him over it; there was no changing his mind. He had shown his dad which way to go with his business, but I could not do the same, though it would have kept it open for another generation. It was his, and it wasn't going anywhere, no matter how much he said he wanted it to. This time, though, *I* was going. That night, I decided it was over for me. I went upstairs and crashed.

CHAPTER 22

How My Funeral Director's License Had a Peaceful, Quiet Death, and I Got My B.S.

D URING THIS TIME, George came to New York to see me. He came to understand that I was a part of him, and I had never trusted, loved, or been so happy and at peace with anyone else before. He was part of my very soul. I only ever rested in his arms, and he felt the same way. Too soon, he went back to Paris to complete his work there.

I went into a depression. My soul just longed for him. I was in agony without him. Our hearse driver, Butch, had a friend who made Italian homemade red and white wine. I bought myself a gallon of each. It was so strong that one glass would just about put me out. I have always been very sensitive to alcohol; it never took a lot to get crocked. Well, the wine was not making me happier, no matter how much I drank.

I was still working, but I was only getting more depressed—to the point where I had to stop working for short periods of time. I couldn't bear it anymore. The dam was beginning to break, and I knew I wouldn't be able to hold back tears that had never been shed for each person who had died, and who I had touched. I felt the loss.

One lesson I learned from this was how honest and true it is that when one person dies, we all die. Every loss is felt throughout humanity like a touch to a spider's web. It vibrates through all of us. We are not fully conscious of it, but that doesn't change the fact. They say a rising tide lifts all boats. I know it has been put in economic terms, but the way I see it, when we rise to reach our own potential, everyone rises. At the Olympics, for example, when one athlete breaks a record or does something previously thought impossible, it only gets easier to break the record again. We all become Olympians.

I wasn't rising, though. I was beginning to drown, and was just holding on by the skin of my teeth. I had a hole in me that only a normal life with George would fill. We knew it was going to be a big change for him, with his medical license, and a change of career for me. We never wrote or talked to each other on the phone. We didn't need to. We just knew, and decided to see how the dust settled when were apart from each other.

Then George returned to New York without telling me he was coming. He just had to come. He called, and we spent time together. Once, he stayed over, and while he was brushing his teeth, his gums bled. I told him to take some vitamin C. I also had some Vitamin

K to help the blood coagulate better. He looked at me and said, "I am a doctor and didn't think of it, and you knew what would heal it." I thought that was great. We both just laughed.

A few days passed, then he said, very seriously, "We could get married. I would have to transfer my medical license to New York, and we could stay here for a couple of years." It sounded great. Then he said, "I want to go back to Lebanon and do what I can to help." I looked at him, looked around the funeral home, and said, "War zone, George?"

He said, "But I will be bringing life into the world." He was an OB-GYN. In other words, he delivered babies as his profession. He would be bringing life into the world, and I would be fully conscious and professionally trained to be aware of death and how it occurred. Like radar. I put my head down, and said, "I can't."

George, like his uncle, Monsignor Shaheen, was far more magnanimous than I was. I had no more to give. If one of the women or children died, I wouldn't be able to easily recoup. The stories about what the war with Syria was doing to people on both sides were too overwhelming for me. I didn't want to slip into an unstoppable, enveloping depression. I was too drained in that area of my life. And what would happen if my drinking went off the deep end because I couldn't handle it? I couldn't marry him with the knowledge there was no way I wasn't going to hit a clinical depression if I wasn't in an environment where I could work it out safely, and that wasn't going to happen with people who had lived through war. I could NEVER do that to George. George left, and I died.

I was still working, but I began to resent the funerals and people's sufferings. The first time, I didn't recognize what it was. The second time it happened, I saw it. I didn't take it out on the family, by any means, but I knew I had to stop, because eventually, *I* would stop functioning. I stopped working. I was so depressed, and couldn't be alone. I went to my parents' house, and cried and cried. I couldn't hold back another tear. Dad took it personally, and began to hate me. He didn't understand, and I couldn't explain it. Rita said, "Laura, come stay with me and Jack. Get away from them, because they are not doing you any good." I had bought *A Course in Miracles* in a bookshop in the Village, and took it to Rita's house.

I watched *Sesame Street* and *Mr. Rogers' Neighborhood*. I started to knit Irish fisherman's sweaters for Rita, Jack, and his sister. I cursed a blue streak while knitting them because the work was so difficult, but it stopped me from crying. *A Course in Miracles* was all about forgiveness. There was a church nearby, and when Lent came around, I went on the retreat they were offering for the week. A priest gave sermons every day. I had time to talk with him about how I was not having an easy time with my chosen career. He told me to read *Man's Search for Meaning*. I did, a number of times, but every time I read it, I just went numb.

I stayed at Rita's for about a year. I guess I was around twenty-six by this time. In that year my Grandmother Jenny died. After that, I went back to work, and hit another depression. This was not working out. I was useless to my father. He told me I would never get a penny from the business, and he wrote me out of it. I went on, even though I prayed for death daily for a very long time.

Friends came by for my birthday to cheer me up with a surprise party. If it had not been for my friend Blanca and her family, I would never have had the strength to go on, or to know unconditional love. She and her brother lived on the third floor across from me and kept me alive with friendship. Blanca told me my dad had told her he didn't want her talking to me. I know because it kept me from focusing on work and only work. He was killing me. She was my friend, and of course paid no attention to that. She came to the party. Pat had a gorilla show up at the door to sing "Happy Birthday" to me. My friends were a riot. They did cheer me up.

After they left, however, there was nothing friends could do. I was suffering from post-traumatic stress, and I knew it. It had started the first time I walked into Bellevue Morgue, and only got worse every time I had to dress a dead body. If I could have hired someone to do that and just work with the families, I would have been fine, but no such luck.

I knew I had been an alcoholic since funeral-directing school, but I couldn't face that fact. When I was a little girl, Dad had taken me to the bar next door, brought me in by the hand, and said, "There is nothing worse in this world than a woman alcoholic." And there I was. I didn't have to drink to know it. I could white-knuckle it and have three drinks a year, but that only made me more miserable because I could not self-medicate against the pain.

I was not a happy camper, and I found myself in a whirlpool of quicksand. Rita and Mom took me to a psychiatrist, and I fought against getting an anti-depressant harder than anything in my life. I was not going to end up taking them if it was the last thing I did, even though I was in agony. I think the shame of it was too much.

It so happened that Joanne had been hospitalized again, and was doing well. The doctors wanted to do a family intervention so we could do what was best for her. I knew how much she was suffering. I wasn't far behind the door. We showed up, sat down, and said hello. Then my father opened his mouth. He said to me, "So, do I sell the business, or not?" I knew this session was for Joanne—why he was bringing this up now was beyond me. I looked him straight in the eye, and said, "Sell it." He got up and walked out. Joanne sat there with her mouth open. Both Mom and I followed him into the elevator, and we all went home. I thought to myself, "No wonder Joanne hates my guts. She must think she doesn't matter to our parents, that only Rita and I matter." I could have killed him.

I gave up. I went to the psychiatrist and went on a low dose of medication. I became able, at this point, to get off the sofa. Things slowly improved for me, but Dad was just getting vicious. He sold the funeral home, but still thought I had left him holding the bag. I eventually got well. I went to Al-Anon, because now that Dad had officially retired, he had started to drink wine. A lot of wine. And I took the brunt of his anger. I learned that alcoholism was a disease, and started detaching in a healthier way, but anger still played a pretty big role with him—anger and denial that I even existed went back and forth with him. Finally, I made a girlfriend in Al-Anon, and we talked about everything. She invited me to go on a retreat with her; she paid. I was dead broke.

On the retreat, it came up that I had been molested in high school. I came back, and applied for Medicaid so I could go to therapy. I knew I needed to air this stuff in an environment where I could see solutions to things that were too overwhelming to carry all at once. I needed to start acting on solutions. I was healing with the structure, unconditional love, and lack of isolation Al-Anon provided.

I had gone on full welfare by now, and was able to move out. In therapy, I eventually got around to telling the therapist about being molested. She looked me in the eye, and said, "Why are you telling me about this? Why aren't you telling the Board of Education?"

"What? Are you kidding me?" I exclaimed.

"No," she replied. I thought to myself, *Yeah, I came here to learn which right actions I needed to take. But this is going too far.* I went home and thought about it, and opened the experience up again. I got so angry I decided she was right. If I didn't do anything about it, nothing was going to change. What if they were doing that to other children, and I continued to do nothing? That was giving them full reign. I would be giving them full permission. I couldn't live with it anymore.

Ironically, I had gotten a phone call from friends now living in California, who told me there was going to be a high school reunion. They asked me to get in touch with whoever I could, because I was still in the neighborhood. I went in the phone book and looked up Mr. Nissen's phone number. I called him up, and told him about it. He was talking like he was all over me again, and then said, "I'm not going, I'm not interested in it."

I said, "Okay, I just called to tell you." I hung up.

I called the Board of Education. They sent two investigators over. I explained everything that had happened. They told me, "Recently, someone called and put up a red flag on Mr. Nissen—that he was stealing money from the baseball team." I didn't know if that was true or not. They took down everything I told them, and said they would get back in touch with me.

At the time, Ed Stancik, lead investigator on the Board of Education, looked like he was dying of cancer, but he was a pit bull toward teachers who had molested children in school. That man did not fool around. He didn't have long to live, and he was making the most of it. I was grateful.

The investigators came back, and said, "The only way we can do anything about this is if you call him up, meet him somewhere with windows so we can videotape it, wear a wire, and get him to talk about it." I think I peed myself in fear, but I said, "Okay, I will." It was an adventure, after all.

They were there when I called him up. We decided the best place to meet was a Dunkin' Donuts near the school, because it had a wall of windows. Mr. Nissen and I made a date to meet. The day came, and so did three or four investigators. One was a woman, and she wrapped me in enough wire to cover a six-foot man a few times over. I had tape and wires all over my back, especially. It was cool outside, so I put on a woolen jacket, and the wires could not be seen. They drove me there in their van, and let me out before we arrived. I walked to the place, and they pulled into one of the parking spots before I got there.

Mr. Nissen was there already, sitting down at a table. He got up when he saw me, and we kissed on the cheek hello. He groaned; I felt sick. We sat down, and talked about how long it had been since we had seen each other. Then he said, "What do you want? Coffee? Any donuts?"

I said, "Sure." I walked in front of him, and he put his hand on my back. I nearly had a heart attack. I moved quickly into the line, and kept my back away from him. All I could think was, *Thank God the woolen jacket is thick enough that he didn't feel the wires*. We got the coffee and some donuts, put them on the table, and started to talk. I said, "Remember how if I failed the Chemistry Regents, you were going to change the grade, because you were marking them?"

"Yeah, but I couldn't mark them, and you passed it on your own," he replied. We started to laugh because it had been a miracle that I passed. We continued to talk about the good old days until he said, "I have to get back to work."

I said, "I am going to stay here and finish my coffee." He smiled at me, and we kissed each other on the cheek with the implied possibility of seeing each other again. His children were grown now, I remembered him saying. He left, and when he was completely out of sight, I went to the van and got in. The lead investigator said, "We got enough to crucify him." Normally, I would have cringed and avoided anything like that—but this time, after years of pain had twisted me into a broken human being, the responsibility I had taken on was being lifted away and put in its rightful place: his shoulders.

I hooked up with a support group made up of other students who had been molested. I found out that five percent of students in every school are, and that statistic only includes the children who have reported. To this day, I write every one of my representatives anytime I get mad about something. Instead of a statute of limitations on when you could take these things to court, I wanted no time limitation. I wrote my governor, who at that time was George Pataki, and told him, "What would you do if your daughter was molested? It can happen to her as easily as it can happen to anyone else. Why is there a statute of limitations?" I didn't think anything about it because writing these letters was just what I did.

About ten o'clock one night, there was a knock on my door. I thought, "Who could that be, so late?" I was in my pajamas. I went to the door and looked through the glass. It was a man and a woman. I said "Yeah, who is it?"

They said, "The FBI."

I said, "What? You have to be kidding me."

"Lady," one of them said, and showed me his badge through the window.

I let them in, saying, "Wait until I get a housecoat." I got one, put it on, and asked, "What do you want?"

He said, "Did you write Governor Pataki?"

"Yeah," I replied. "So?"

He said, "Do you realize it was a threat?"

"A threat? Here, look, look at all these letters I have been writing because I was molested. I didn't threaten him, I told him the truth. It happens to so many people. Why is his daughter so special, that it can't happen to her?" Then I got scared and said, "You think I was going to do it?" I just shut my mouth. They looked at the stuff, and saw that I wasn't lying and was just trying to be a good citizen.

"Okay," they said, and left. I thought to myself, *Holy crap, it would be me who has the FBI come to my door.* Governor Pataki changed the statute of limitations from five years to two, instead of raising it to more years or implementing no time limitation. I believe in karma, and I know that somewhere, somehow, somebody fucked him good. I don't have a problem with it. I told the Board of Ed about what Bert had done, but they said, "Because it happened off school grounds, we can't do anything about it." Because I had told them about it, I left a red flag for Bert at the Board of Education, and was ready to be a character witness for the rest of my life. I shook the dust off my heels, and never had another drink again or smoked another joint.

I knew, however, that it still had a terrible effect on me when I married at thirty-two, and when I had my Robert at thirty-three.

Right after Robert was born, my Grandmother Josephine died. She called me beforehand and said, "I want to leave you one of the chairs." I told her, "I don't want a chair, Grandma," and we started to argue about it. Then I said to her, "I want you to stay." I used to say that all the time—that I didn't want her to die, but to stay around. Grandma Josephine's re-

THE UNDERTAKER

sponse was always, "What do you want to do, stuff me and put me on a shelf?" I would look like I was thinking about it, joking that as a funeral director, I probably could. Then she would mumble something under her breath that I was glad I never understood—but she had a smile on her face when she did it. Then I'd laugh. When I told her this time that I didn't want her to leave, no one laughed. She thought about it, and said "Okay." Then we said goodbye, and she hung up the phone.

Grandma died of congestive heart failure at ninety. As I was closing her casket, one of the pallbearers said, "Wow, what beautiful ankles she has." I slammed the casket closed and said, "What are you doing looking at my grandmother's ankles?" Then I laughed, and said to her out loud, "Grandma, is this your idea of loving 'em and leaving 'em? Only you could pull something like that off."

Right after she was buried, every single plant in my apartment bloomed—even a cactus I had never known could bloom. Grandma used to call me Sunshine, but by this point, she was literally sunshine herself. I still smile when I think about how lucky I am to have had someone like that as my grandmother.

Six months later, my sister Rita died at forty from lung cancer. It wasn't the cancer that got her, though—it was the infection she picked up at the hospital that killed her. Soon after that, I was divorced at thirty-four. I found out that it can take up to twenty-five years after a molestation occurs to be able to face it and look at the devastation it caused in your life, let alone talk to anyone about it.

289

I did meet Mr. Nissen again, though. I decided, one day, to visit my parents and bring bagels; my mom always wanted to see me. I was in line outside when guess who should walk out of the bagel store right into me? "Ms. Del Gaudio," he said.

"Mr. Nissen." There was an awkward pause, so I said with a smile, "Didn't you always say I was the best student you ever had?" He didn't say a word, and apparently found it easier to leave me alone. Actually, he found it easier to leave all the students alone. The Board of Ed had stopped him from teaching. They took him out of the classroom and gave him a desk job. I was so angry that that was all they had done, but looking back, he did lose his job, and never to my knowledge did it again. I had taken on his guilt when I was seventeen years old, and put it back where it belonged when I was forty.

I had kept up payments to keep my funeral director's license active, thinking I could go back to it, even just to run funerals for some extra money—but I just couldn't bring myself to do it. I forgot to pay to renew it one year, and realized much later that it had died a quiet and peaceful death.

I figured I was only thirty credits away, and if I wiped out all non-transferable courses, I could get a Bachelor of Science in Funeral Service Administration. If I had a degree, it didn't matter what it was in—I still had a degree. I had fulfilled the requirement. If I wanted to return, all I had to do was make up the required yearly credits. No big deal. Up until then, I knew I would never take them. This time, though, there was nothing holding me back. I wanted to see just how stupid I was. I pulled straight As. Not so stupid after all. By that time, my father was dying. One of my last classes was a Business Management course. I was in my forties, and in school with twenty-year-olds. One of the assignments was to interview a parent about work: why they had gone into it, the kind of job they had done, etc. I figured, *why not?* I would interview my father. I knew he had loved the business, and it would be nice for us to have one last talk about it before he died. I wrote an interesting interview, and got an A on it.

But it was more than that. My dad kept calling me a son of a bitch before the interview, and I had gotten so tired of it. One day, very quietly, I said to him, "You know, Leo, I know you're not stupid. Can't you see that I am not a son of a bitch, I am a daughter of a bastard? When are you going to get that?"

He thought about that for a while. He always thought about things when I called him Leo. After the interview, he said to me, "You wouldn't have left if I had spoken nicer to you."

In my gentle, pleasant way, I said, "No shit!"

"Your mother told me you left because it made you sick. It is too late to change anything; I didn't leave you a penny." I didn't say a word. He was too close to dying. "I would never have done it if I knew." I knew what he meant: taking it out on me. It was his way of apologizing, and I fully accepted it and forgave him. Why not? I loved him. I could never help myself when it came to that. He said, "As far as the money goes, let the chips fall where they may."

A little while later, he told me he still loved his sister. And then he died.

I had gotten my daddy back.

Laura Del Gaudio

While doing word research for a title for this book, I wanted to be as honest as I could, because I have found my profession.

A "writer" was originally referred to as an "under-taker." *I was meant to be one.*

"Dance me to the end of love."

— LEONARD COHEN

In Memoriam
Rita Raber
Diane Lewis

DISCUSSION GUIDE

1. Laura Del Gaudio's memoir is a journey in time in an Italian, family-run funeral business. Throughout the memoir Laura talks about her home life and various family members. In today's society do you see anything similar; if so what?

2. The memoir is very family rooted in one place (New York), with a few exceptions. How does the author characterize her home city?

3. How does the Del Gaudio's Italian culture influence the stories Laura tells?

4. The author speaks openly about depression, abuse, addiction, and suicide. Were such things spoken about openly in Laura's family growing up? How has communication around these issues changed? How has it not?

5. Laura also speaks frankly about mental illness, from her own experiences, her father's and her sister's. Why

is it important to create an open and honest dialogue about mental illness? How was the way this issue is treated changed over the years, from her father's upbringing, to her own, to today's?

6. What has been your experience with loss/grief, if any? Would getting the type of help that the author offered help you?

7. How are undertakers often portrayed in literature and other media? How is Laura similar to them? How is she different?

8. What events contributed to the author to hit her lowest and her highest points? Do you think Laura found peace at the end of the story?

RESOURCES

It is better to be heard than suffer in silence.

If you or someone you know is in crisis or distress, please refer to these resources:

Dial 311 in New York
National Suicide Hotline   800-273-8255
National Domestic Hotline   800-799-7233
Child Abuse Hotline   800 4 A CHILD   800-422-4453
National Alliance for the Mentally Ill (NAMI)   800-950-6264

A portion of the author's profits

from the sale of this book

will be donated to

St. Jude's Research Hospital.